High-Technology Degree Alternatives

Earning A High-Tech Degree While Working Full Time

Joel Butler

Professional Publications, Inc.
Belmont, CA

HIGH-TECHNOLOGY DEGREE ALTERNATIVES

Printed in the United States of America

ISBN: 0-912045-61-2

Professional Publications, Inc.
1250 Fifth Avenue, Belmont, CA 94002
(415) 593-9119

Current printing of this edition: 2

Library of Congress Cataloging-in-Publication Data

Butler, Joel, 1956-
      High-technology degree alternatives : earning a high-tech degree
while working full time / Joel Butler.
            p.   cm.
      Includes index.
      ISBN 0-912045-61-2
      1. Technical education--United States. 2. Non-formal education-
-United States. 3. University extension--United States.
      4. Degrees, Academic--United States.   I. Title.
      T73.B895   1994
      607'. 1'173--dc20   93-85502
                                                                                        CIP

Table of Contents

Preface vii

Acknowledgments xiii

Chapter One
Better Ways to Earn Technology Degrees 1
    Typical Back-to-School Method No. 1: Quitting Work 2
    Typical Back-to-School Method No. 2: Keep Your Job 3
    Accredited Alternatives: Legitimate and Essential 3

Chapter Two
Three Steps to Discover Which High-Tech Degree You Need 5
    Step One: Define Underlying Goals 5
    Step Two: Choose Your Degree, Major, and Target Graduation Date 7
    Step Three: Set Initial Deadlines to Start Off Right..................................10

Chapter Three
The Basics of a Faster, Easier Degree Program.......................................13
    Degrees from Nontraditional Schools Save Money and Time 13
    Ten Ways to Pick Up More College Credits 15
    How to Choose Between the Two Types of Nontraditional Schools 18

Chapter Four
When to Use Traditional Classroom Study...23

Chapter Five
Fail-Safe Credit Transfers 27
    Transfer Previously Earned Credits to Your New School 27
    Making Sure All Your Future Credits Transfer 30

Chapter Six
Independent Study Courses as Close as Your Own Mailbox...................33
    New Methods of Independent Study 35
    Other Aspects of Independent Study 36

Chapter Seven
Cut Your Degree Completion Time with Exams 39
    Using Challenge Examinations for Course Credit 39
    Earn Large Blocks of Credit Through Standardized Exams 42
    Skip One Year of College with Five CLEP Exams 47
    Use AP Exams to Bypass College Courses 49
    Earn One-Fourth of a Degree from a GRE Subject Exam 51
    Course Credits from ACT PEP Exams 53
    Use DANTES Exams to Avoid Classes 55
    Other Exams to Get Your Degree Sooner 56

Chapter Eight
College Credits from Training You've Already Received 59
   Turn Company-Sponsored Training into College Credits 59
   Earn Credit from Professional Certificates and Licenses 62
   Credit Awards from Military Training and Service Ratings 64

Chapter Nine
Turn What You Know into College Credits 69
   Prior Learning and Portfolio Assessment 69

Chapter Ten
Create Your Own College Courses and Custom Degree Programs 75
   Individualized Degree Programs 75
   Look for New and Obscure Ways to Earn Credit 77

Chapter Eleven
Focus on Key Methods to Improve Credit-Earning Efforts 79
   Should You Choose Your School First? 79
   Estimate How Much Credit You Already Have 80

Chapter Twelve
Strengthen Your Degree Plans by Choosing the Right School 83
   Survey, Study, and Sift Colleges and Universities 83
   Shortening the List 85
   School Selection: The Final Cut 91

Chapter Thirteen
Create Your Degree Sketch 93
   What Does a Degree Sketch Look Like? 93
   Degree Sketch Format and Content 95
   Rearrange Your Credit Inventory for Maximum Usage 100

Chapter Fourteen
Get a Head Start When You're Admitted 107
   Getting Accepted Is Usually Painless 107
   Make the Most of Your Time During the Admission Process 108
   Your Degree Plan: Seeking Approval 109

Chapter Fifteen
Getting to Graduation Day Using the Degree Plan 113
   Lessen the Impact of Changes in Plans 113
   Doing Well and Meeting Your Goals 114
   Gradual Steps to Graduation 115
   The Big Day: Commencement 117

Chapter Sixteen
Realize Your Goals: What to Do After Graduation 119
   Achieve Your Goals Through Self-Promotion 119
   Review Your Goals and Monitor Achievements 120

Appendix A
Glossary 123

Appendix B
Colleges and Universities 125

Appendix C
Accreditation 163

Appendix D
Obtaining a High School Diploma 169

Appendix E
Career and Job-Hunting Information Leads 171

Appendix F
Help from University Degree Advisory 175

Appendix G
Bibliography and Resources 177

Index 179

Doug and the Elusive Degree

Throughout his youth, Doug seemed destined to work in the electronics field; he did well in science and math and always gave new life to old, broken radios and televisions. Unfortunately, his likelihood of completing a four- or five-year electronics degree seemed poor because his family couldn't afford it. The Air Force appeared to be a reasonable option because Doug could take advantage of its training as well as earn post-discharge educational benefits.

After enlisting, Doug excelled in electronics training and performed notably in his work assignments, which primarily involved maintaining radar and electronic test equipment. Unfortunately, after he left the service, Doug's training and experience didn't put him on equal footing with people holding college degrees. Doug eventually joined a good electronics company, but his technician-type manufacturing assignments were low in status and unchallenging. Doug planned to show his employer what he could do and had faith that he would be recognized and rewarded.

Soon Doug married, started a family, and began to feel an urgency to examine his career path. His performance reviews came every six months filled with glowing comments, and Doug usually was called on for difficult or critical assignments. He decided he could move up by transferring to the engineering department, which looked like a great place to work and had more potential for advancement.

Competition for openings in the engineering department was stiff, but eventually Doug's reputation as a quick learner and hard worker earned him a transfer. His title was still technician, but he learned much from working with degreed design engineers. Although Doug received performance reviews that rated him as above average or outstanding, his manager made it clear that in order to be promoted to a real engineering position Doug needed to obtain his college degree. Doug thought another company would be more interested in his proven abilities, so he applied for various design positions and sent out dozens of résumés. After receiving no responses, he realized what he had to do and enrolled part time at a nearby university.

Doug found that the university also refused to recognize his previous training or learning from experience. The educational path he had to follow to complete his degree included more than six continuous years of classroom attendance. Because of Doug's training and experience, he already knew much of the material in his required electronics courses. Doug realized that nothing would prevent the university from treating him like a typical 18-year-old student.

Work and family commitments forced Doug to delay taking courses, and occasionally he had to withdraw from a class. Because of his slow progress, Doug wished for an easier way to complete a degree.

Today, when Doug sees a help-wanted ad for an enticing position, he might send out a résumé, but when he interviews, his lack of a college degree seems to cloud the discussion. A stalled career combined with the dreary prospect for degree completion is giving Doug a consistent message: His career peaked before age 30.

Linda Finds an Answer

Shortly after high school graduation, Linda had two dynamite job offers, each with real long-term career potential. One position was with an airline; the other with a large telecommunications company. Linda always knew she would get a college degree, but she felt the two great opportunities would give her a four-year career head start over her high school peers. She accepted the offer from the telecommunications company and began an information processing and communications career.

Linda made a good choice because her company provided her with interesting work and accommodated some of her other priorities over the years. For example, she was able to raise her two sons by taking extended maternity leaves and working part time in the company's network operations headquarters.

Along the way, Linda participated in corporate-sponsored training as well as taking a potpourri of courses related to the degree that she would one day complete. She always believed a degree was important, and she realized she would be further along in her career with a college diploma. With her desire for a degree intact, Linda determined the issue wasn't if, but how, she would complete the degree.

Her work position and responsibility had grown over the years within a department that truly defined the look, feel, and experience of high technology. Her job satisfaction was high, so she didn't want to quit work to go back to school. What Linda needed was an educational alternative to college that catered to her needs. She had another concern about an accelerated degree program: Why should she labor for five or more years if she'd already proven herself in many areas?

During Linda's search for an educational alternative, her company arranged for a nontraditional college to give an orientation session to interested employees. Linda attended the presentation, and as she listened to what the college offered, it became clear that she'd found the answer: This school marketed itself to people like her; her educational experience would be totally different from that at traditional schools. At the non-traditional school, coordinators and advisors worked with students to provide a focus for communication; different methods of earning credit promised convenience, time savings, and the ability to translate Linda's experience-based learning into college-level credits.

With the support of her company (but while still working full time), Linda enrolled in a nontraditional program with the goal of obtaining a bachelor's degree in business data processing. Making use of innovative and stimulating credit-building methods, Linda attended very few classes; gaining most of her credit through the evaluation of her work-based learning, corporate training courses, and standardized exams. Linda received her associate's degree in business data processing slightly more than a year after enrollment. She obtained her bachelor's degree in approximately 18 more months. Linda's success was due to determination, as well as taking the time to understand how the nontraditional degree process worked at her school.

Today, promotions and higher salaries are not Linda's only goals. She has the ability to make a career change and is considering part-time teaching to enhance her existing career. She knows that without her college-level degree her chances for success in this area would be slim to none. Linda says, "The only security you have is between your ears." She believes that her degree has given her a new sense of confidence and marketability.

What this Book Can Do for You

The preceding examples demonstrate that you can earn a college degree in ways that are easier, quicker, cheaper, and more satisfying than you probably believe possible.

Once Doug realized the importance of attaining a degree, he experienced the ultimate frustration: The university was forcing a purposeful and skilled adult into a program designed for high school graduates. If you read Linda's story first and then read what Doug went through, you might be tempted to call him to say, "Don't give up hope, there's a better way!"

If you desire a high-technology degrees at the associate, bachelor, or graduate level, this book will help you accomplish the following.

- You can drastically cut the time it takes to reach graduation.
- You can reduce the cost of completing an education.
- You can eliminate the need to complete unnecessary coursework.
- You can transfer all your previous college work to a new school.
- You can turn military experience into instant college credits.
- You can earn college credit for learning as a result of hands-on experience.
- You can accumulate large blocks of credit without ever entering a classroom.
- You can design your own college degree program.
- You can design your own college coursework and study plans.
- You can take short exams to earn large amounts of credit.
- You can ease the reentry process if you've been away from school.
- You can gain admission to a good school regardless of previous school experience.
- You can work any or all of the preceding into an already-busy life.

If this sounds like a different world, it is: It's the world of nontraditional colleges and universities. The odd thing is that these alternatives are not rare; they're available to anyone, anywhere. Perhaps one day these accredited alternatives to traditional degree programs will be simple to understand and widely promoted, but today they are often an obscure jumble of academic jargon and policies. This book is a guide to the process of discovering, understanding, and using alternatives to traditional colleges and universities.

The Stories You Are About to Read Are True

A significant part of this book is based on the experiences of people who have actually earned their degrees from alternative schools. You'll find those experiences shared in quotes, stories, and anecdotes. Many of the people I interviewed preferred to keep their privacy intact. To honor that desire and to maintain continuity of presentation, I've removed or obscured name references. However, these stories are genuine firsthand accounts of the experiences you're likely to encounter.

Joel Butler
October 1993

Acknowledgments

Portions of the information on financial aid and job hunting are derived from the Bureau of Labor's *Occupational Outlook Handbook*.

The inclusion of information about schools, testing services, publications, and other organizations doesn't constitute their implied endorsement of this publication, nor does it imply their review of it.

For their assistance, direction, and information, thank you to the following contributors: Linda Beedie-Grashorn, Julie Clayton, Jonathan Clemens, Joyce Empie, Amy Foust, Linda Headlee-Walker, Linda Holt, Wendall Kenner, Maureen Lancaster, Leo J. LeBrut, David Lutz, Jim McGrath, Margaret Mirabelli, Evelyn Rowe, Erin Sneller, Carol Stallone, and Kent Warren.

Many thanks to Nancy A. Gubka for her considerable knowledge of postsecondary education, as well as her excellent editorial eye.

For their timely advice, inspiration, and encouragement, thank you to Cathy Baron, Gerry Galbo, Guy Kawasaki, J.G. Milanowski, S.J. Saullo, Donnie Savage, Ken Sedgwick, Jason Standifer, Val Stentz, Mark Stephenson, Greg Strockbine, Paul Teich, Nick Tsacamoungas, and Renee Wildman.

Finally, special thanks to Random Butler and Cameron Butler. They waited patiently for Dad to finish this book.

Better Ways to Earn Technology Degrees

If your career goals include continuous advancement, you can't have too many degrees. Does that overstate the importance of your education? Perhaps, but many of us have gone job-hunting wishing our résumés had more credentials listed under the Educational Background section. Also, consider this: If promotions are based only on competent work, why is it possible for valuable employees to be continually passed over because others have more diplomas on their walls?

Like it or not, you must eventually accept that employers develop quick ways to separate qualified job applicants from those who might not be qualified; degrees, or the lack of degrees, are one such criteria. Granted, in any hasty separation process, some diamonds will be thrown out with the dirt, but that's a risk most hiring managers take when they have one job opening and dozens of applicants to consider. This practice shows no sign of going away, despite the fact that most experienced managers have, at times, worked with highly educated incompetents.

In all high-tech professions, it's easy to find outstanding technical contributors who are being ignored because they lack certain degrees. As a technical manager, I've seen many of these people distinguish themselves as skilled professionals who consistently do the same work as formally degreed coworkers. However, for these people, career conditions are usually different.

- After they reach a certain level, career progress will stop. Job opportunities at other companies will be limited.
- Their stature in the company will be lower: smaller salaries as well as lesser job titles and positions.
- If they are laid off, subsequent job searching will take longer, with less chance of finding an equivalent opportunity.

Acquiring the necessary degree can change all these conditions. In fact, obtaining a degree may not make people more qualified, but suddenly the world thinks so—new promotions and outside job offers may seem to pour in. As the Wizard of Oz wisely realized, the Scarecrow didn't need brains, he only needed a diploma to officially certify the intelligence he already demonstrated.

Will this book help you beat the system? No, but it will show you that college degrees can be obtained without great investments of time and money. You will learn that college credits can be earned outside the classroom. This book is intended to help technical professionals earn accredited technical degrees at the associate, bachelor, and graduate levels. Success in obtaining technical degrees can result in promotions, outside job offers, increased career security, and a sense of achievement.

If this sounds too good to be true, also consider that all degree alternatives presented here are legitimate. All college programs described are regionally accredited by the same agencies that certify well-known traditional schools such as MIT, Harvard, and Stanford. The American Council on Education refers to these alternatives as nontraditional education. Today, tens of thousands of students are benefiting from accredited nontraditional education. Graduates of nontraditional schools use their degrees to enhance their careers and even to gain entrance to traditional graduate schools.

However, degree alternatives are not for everyone. Nontraditional approaches rely on self-motivated students and work best when the students already have considerable experience and/or previous college work. Those with plans to attain admission to a top graduate school should consider that the prestige factor of some nontraditional schools may not match the best of the traditionals. Still, to understand why many people are turning to alternatives for high-tech degrees, a review of traditional methods is helpful.

Typical Back-to-School Method No. 1: Quitting Work

It would be ideal to drop everything and go back to school (this singular goal increases your chance of completion and successful graduation), but this method is an unthinkable luxury for most working adults since leaving behind a career means leaving behind an income. However, even if money isn't an issue, there are other considerations.

Putting a career on hold for years is a questionable move, especially in technology-oriented companies. Hands-on exposure to new developments is more likely to occur in the commercial environment. I worked with a computer engineer who resigned to pursue his master's and doctorate at Tulane University. Before long, he was back in the office during his vacations and other breaks to help out with various projects. In addition to the extra

---

KEEP UP WITH TECHNOLOGY

From the *Occupational Outlook Handbook*, published by the Bureau of Labor:

"Engineers in high-technology fields such as electronics may find that their knowledge becomes obsolete rapidly. Engineers who employers consider not to have kept up may find themselves passed over for promotions and are particularly vulnerable to layoffs. On the other hand, it is often these high-technology areas that offer the greatest challenges, the most interesting work, and the highest salaries."

pay, he liked having something real to sink his teeth into. He recognized a major flaw in the "drop everything" approach: It may not be realistic to return after a few years of school and expect to pick up a high-tech career where it was left off.

Another interesting phenomenon is that many adults find a full-time return to school unsettling. Many aspects tend to grate: the elementary nature of some required classes, the rigidness of degree programs, the lack of recognition of existing knowledge, and the social discord of being among a large population of young adults.

Typical Back-to-School Method No. 2 : Keep Your Job

Traditional colleges have been aggressively marketing fast-track programs for adult students. Evening and weekend classes can lead people to many types of degrees. This has become such a viable business that numerous schools have been started specifically to serve this need. But just how fast are these fast-track programs? Typical MBA programs can be completed in two years if you're willing to take on a full load for the entire duration. The catch here is that it's almost impossible to sustain this amount of schoolwork while you have a job. Three to five years is more realistic, if you can stick with this extended period of study. In general, the more demanding your work is, the longer it takes to complete a degree. Unfortunately, high-tech positions rank among the most demanding.

One of the most important factors affecting the likelihood of your graduation is the time it takes to complete your degree. Increasing this time period decreases your prospects for completion. Many "drop nothing" students discover they cannot complete these longer periods of study because of job pressures, transfers, or weariness. Obviously, some people complete these types of programs, but for those considering this degree option, ask each school what percentage of people enrolling eventually graduate

Accredited Alternatives: Legitimate and Essential

Much of the information in these pages was gathered as part of my degree-consulting work with individuals investigating nontraditional education. Many of my clients knew their employers would promote them if they could finish their degrees, some wanted to find new employers but felt degrees were required, and others wanted to use degrees to switch careers. Common to all the people I've worked with is a desire for personal achievement and self-satisfaction. This leads to some thoughts on why the alternative of accredited nontraditional education is not only legitimate, but necessary.

A suspicious attitude toward high-tech degree alternatives is understandable, but hardly appropriate. There are colleges that will award a year of computer science credits for passing a single three-hour exam. Does this mean the nontraditional students who take advantage of this are getting away with something? After all, they aren't going to classes or spending large sums of money.

To answer this question: No college or university would risk its valued accreditation by handing out degrees to the undeserving. In fact, nontraditional degree programs are usually offered as an outreach by well-known traditional colleges and universities, including state-run university systems and private educational institutions. Nontraditional programs simply recognize that people can gain knowledge outside the classroom. If the learning experience is equivalent to what is taught in the classroom, then credit deserves to be awarded.

You must reject the common belief that obtaining a degree is one part learning, one part endurance test, and one part financial burden. Is it necessary to withhold education and credentials because of work and family obligations? Can we afford to thwart the career goals of capable lower-income people? Nontraditional education is not only legitimate, but is another way our society helps many individuals become more fulfilled and productive. The value of nontraditional education is realized every day. People are more content and productive if recognized for their worth and challenged accordingly. The advice here is meant to improve your career and help you gain self-satisfaction. Use it for these ends, and your present and future employers will benefit as well.

BIBLIOTHECA

In addition to this book, the most important resource you'll need is your local library. Seek out one that has a large reference section and a ready, helpful staff. If you have a reasonably large college near you, also try its library.

Creating a list of books you need before you go to the library can be a real time-saver. If you can't find a book you want, try to get it from the interlibrary loan program (ask a librarian for details).

Also, many libraries have installed electronic card catalogs and on-line information databases that personal computer users can access from home via modem.

If you haven't been to the library in a long time, simply step back in and ask a librarian for help.

Three Steps to Discover Which High-Tech Degree You Need

The idea that a degree can be obtained with less expense of time and money can be so captivating that many want to dive right into the process without doing some initial groundwork. This groundwork includes understanding your motivations for gaining educational credentials and then settling on a degree appropriate to those goals. This chapter will be your guide through these initial steps of discovering your own reasons for wanting a degree and choosing the right degree program. For those with the urge to push forward, consider the Chinese proverb that says, "If you don't know where you're going, any road will do." As with any worthy goal, identifying what motivates you to pursue a technical degree is important in building an appropriate, achievable degree plan.

Step One: Define Underlying Goals

To begin, you need to identify the fundamental reasons for wanting a college degree. There are many career-oriented motivations for attaining technical degrees. Job security and salary are just two areas that can improve as a result of earning an accredited college degree. However, not all motivations are career related; many technical professionals desire educational credentials for achievement and personal satisfaction.

It's a common mistake to focus on a target date for degree completion or on the actual physical diploma as primary motivations. These may fail to get you through the roadblocks and detours you will likely encounter. The best way to persevere through the entire journey is to keep in mind what you want your degree to do for you. Goal-setting helps you to maintain this focus.

There are many motivational books on the market, so it's likely that you've already been exposed to the concepts of goals and goal-setting. Because of the overabundance of these books, many people actively avoid further exposure to the subject. Even so, there is validity to the technique of goal-setting when used to attain technical degrees. However, you don't need to adopt goal-setting as a sacred, obsessive practice that governs every aspect of your life.

The simplified approach to goal-setting is:

- Determine specific goals with completion times.
- Write those goals down.
- Review and adjust goals at regular intervals.

One way to find your goals is to view a college degree as a means to an end: Find out what you want educational credentials (a degree) to do for you.

The benefits of a college degree can be divided into the two areas of personal and career growth. However, in modern society, career and self-worth can be virtually synonymous. This is proven when you realize that your own motivations for attaining a degree probably fall into both areas. After all, most of us would expect to experience a feeling of personal satisfaction from a career promotion and/or salary increase. Self-assessment based on your career is a tested way to arrive at internal motivations. The following is a typical example of that method.

■ ■ ■

Example: Find Your Motivations

Consider the digital hardware technician who, after 10 years of experience, reflects back on that career and then looks into the future. It is quite possible that this technician has attained the highest position possible in the company for someone without a bachelor's degree. Although the pay is OK, it may be disheartening to work shoulder-to-shoulder with degreed design engineers, often covering for their mistakes. When you also consider the little extras available to degreed design engineers, the subtle message of status difference becomes evident. This reflection may lead to the following motivation: "I need to increase my self-worth by increasing my status within this company. A role as a degreed design engineer is what I want."

• • • • •

This is just one example of exploring motivation to set goals. There are probably as many different reasons for pursuing a degree as there are people wanting degrees. Reflection is a simple technique by which you can arrive at your own set of goals. Before you determine which degrees will help you attain your goals, you must consider another side of motivation: fear.

Does Fear Encourage Achievement?

In technical professions, things are generally getting tougher for those without degrees. Many young people are graduating from

POSSIBLE BENEFITS RESULTING FROM A COLLEGE DEGREE

- Entry into a new or changed profession
- Promotions and salary increases from your current employer
- Greater job security
- Better and different job assignments
- Enhanced status among coworkers
- Ability to pursue further higher education
- Get out from under the dark cloud of the non-degreed
- Becoming smarter through learning
- Official recognition for existing knowledge and skills
- Satisfaction from settling unfinished education
- Opened opportunities at other companies
- Personal achievement and self-satisfaction
- Increased self-confidence
- Additional respect from family and friends
- Become an educational role model for your children
- Show some snob that you too can earn a degree
- Something new with which to decorate the wall

college with technical degrees. In the world of high technology, competition from abroad arises not only from foreign companies, but also from foreign nationals with excellent educational credentials looking for work outside their own countries. Plus, many degreed high-tech employees are going back for advanced graduate degrees. To borrow a saying, "The neighborhood is getting smaller and the bullies are getting bigger."

But the intent here is not to fan the flames of fear (or of nationalism); in fact, the message is the exact opposite: Fear doesn't have to be your primary motivator. A college degree puts substantial positive force behind the desire for career and personal growth. Some people have successfully used this motivation: "I'd better get a degree or I might be the first to go during a layoff." This is just a more immediate statement about enhanced job security. For some, a little anxiety may be useful, but terror is usually counterproductive to the degree-completion process.

Using Degrees to Increase Your Income

Since it's hard to pretend that most people choose personal satisfaction over earning potential as a motivator, consider the issue of monetary payback. Career motivation experts say salary is only a short-term incentive, but this doesn't stop many people from wanting to continually increase their earnings over the course of a long career. Many people find it hard to work effectively when they believe they are underpaid.

You've been taught that education is the key to higher pay. It has been estimated that for a degree that prepares you for an advanced profession, every year of education completed increases your earnings by an average of 7 percent. Census Bureau data from 1990 shows that a bachelor's degree in engineering nets the average holder $2,953 per month, while the average high school graduate earns just $1,077 per month.

Step Two: Choose Your Degree, Major, and Target Graduation Date

Look at the goals you've written down, then try to ascertain the type of degree that would help you achieve them. Specifically, what you are attempting to discover is:

- The level of degree you need: associate's, bachelor, or graduate
- The degree major, such as electrical engineering, mechanical engineering, data processing, or computer science
- An optional area of core study, such as digital hardware design, fluid dynamics, or artificial intelligence

Degrees are often referred to with initials. For example, B.S.C.S., BSCS, and B.Sci.CS all refer to a bachelor of science degree in computer science. Various other technical degrees occur at the associate, bachelor, and master levels in many study disciplines.

The Difference Between a Science Degree and an Arts Degree

Many people wonder what the difference is between a bachelor of science and a bachelor of arts degree. A specific concern is that in technical occupations, a BA might not be as highly regarded as a BS in the same area of study (for example, there are certain schools that offer both a BA and a BS in Computer Science). As one might expect, the real difference between the two degrees is small. An arts degree usually has a slightly greater liberal arts requirement, meaning more required credits in humanities, social science, history, general science, and perhaps foreign language. A BS degree may require one to four more courses than an arts degree.

If there is not much real difference, how might the holder of an arts degree be perceived as different? First, in technical professions, there is some bias favoring science degrees over arts degrees. Second, recruiters in personnel departments are sometimes reduced to filtering good from bad candidates. They can do this filtering without having to think: they simply compare credentials of applicants (from their résumés or applications) to the job descriptions written by the hiring manager. A job description may have an educational background section that requires a BSCS or equivalent. In a robot-like filtering process, "BSCS or equivalent" might be effectively reduced to BSCS, so someone with a BA in computer science would not be considered.

In high-tech professions, the safe choice is a science degree. This is usually easy to find when choosing a college and degree program. (As a bonus, you might not have to learn Russian.) Overall, BA and BS degrees are of more concern to those with little or no work experience at jobs where educational credentials are the most important part of determining qualification.

The Educational Credential Target

If you are experienced, how important is having the right degree? Do you need an exact match, or can you get away with any degree? There is no hard and fast rule, but the ranking most personnel

DISCOVER YOUR MOTIVATION

Do some self-exploration and discover what you want educational credentials to do for you. These are your motivations for completing a degree. Write them down. Remember that the degree itself should not be a motivator.

recruiters and hiring managers use is shown by the following target. Imagine that the position to be filled requires a bachelor's degree in computer science or the equivalent.

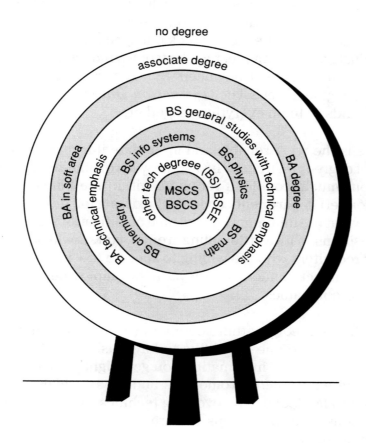

The Educational Credential Target
Job Titles Requiring a BSCS

Ways to Find Out Which Degrees Are Needed for Career Goals

Those working in the high-tech industry may already know what degrees are required for advancement. If not, there are many available sources that will help.

- Bureau of Labor's *Occupational Outlook Handbook*
- Current employer job descriptions
- Potential employer job descriptions
- People already holding the job you want
- Professional recruiters
- College advisors and counselors
- Help-wanted advertisements

✓ **RECORD YOUR OBJECTIVES**

Write down on paper all the information you've obtained about your goals and desired educational credentials. Decide what specific degree you need to achieve your goals. On the same piece of paper, write down the specific degree you will need to meet those goals.

The Bureau of Labor publishes the *Occupational Outlook Handbook*, a comprehensive look at U.S. employment in both quantitative and qualitative senses. Within each career category are typical training and educational credentials. The *Handbook* is in most library reference sections. Although high-technology professions are covered, it can be hard to pick out specific professions within an industry. For example, the electronics industry makes distinctions among different engineers by expertise: digital engineers, analog engineers, etc. The *Occupation Outlook Handbook*, however, tends to lump everything together.

Where is the most reliable and up-to-date information about the type of degree you'll need? Inside the walls of high-tech businesses. Without much trouble, a recruiter within the human resources (personnel) department can look at existing job descriptions that detail what the minimum educational qualifications are for technical positions. With a little calling around, you should be able to find a few recruiters who are willing to spend a few minutes with you on this subject. Remember, they are the employment sales forces for their companies.

If you find someone within a company (even your own) who holds a title similar to one you'd like to have, ask that person to help well. However, the information you get might be dated. Look for someone with recent promotions and an awareness of what is needed to land jobs in an evolving technical world. For a variety of reasons, it always helps to form these type of professional acquaintances.

Forward-projecting information about employment and educational credentials can also be obtained from advisors at local colleges and universities. Schools are always under pressure to produce graduates with up-to-date knowledge and skills (even though colleges have a hard time reacting as quickly as technological employers would like). Another similar resource is high school guidance offices. You probably won't find people in these offices eager to assist you; most academic personnel are performing multiple roles and don't have time to talk with everyone. When you do find willing help, be prepared to accommodate their time constraints.

Step Three: Set Initial Deadlines

After you identify your motivations and determine what specific degree will be needed, the next step is to set deadlines for achievement and commit them to paper. Your ability to determine reasonable deadlines will improve as you read the following

---

THE SHORT JOURNEY BEGINS WITH...

A nuclear navy school safety officer earned his bachelor of science degree through a non-traditional school and now promotes alternative degree options at his base. After helping dozens of other active personnel into degree programs, he notes,

"The hardest move in the world is getting started. Once they get started, they're ready to go, they're in automatic, they're going to finish their degree."

chapters and begin contacting colleges, so don't worry. Review and adjustment are part of a goal-oriented process. Future changes in your plan don't obviate the immediate need to establish milestones for degree attainment. Putting goals on paper has a significance of its own: It is the standard by which people are held accountable in contract situations, and it seems to work for individual goals as well.

Another aspect of making and meeting goals involves enlisting help. Meeting any goal may require the aid of family, friends, and employers. Some people find additional help making goals through external stimuli. If this is the case for you, then by all means announce your intentions to people in your life.

SUMMARY

If you've followed the three steps in this chapter, you have committed to paper the most important aspects of any degree attainment effort: what specific degree you need to help you attain your goals, and when you want to attain that degree. Following are the three steps in brief.

1. Define your goals: You've identified what you expect a degree to do for you.

2. Select a specific degree: With research, you've determined what specific degree will help achieve the goals you've defined.

3. Specify an initial deadline for achievement: This is your first guess about when you'll finish your degree. Even though it might be far in the future, it is important to begin this phase of accountability now, with the understanding it may be changed later.

The Basics of a Faster, Easier Degree Program

Alternatives to traditional study may be difficult to grasp, especially if you begin by reading catalogs and bulletins sent out by nontraditional schools. In these promotional materials, you often don't get a frame of reference for many of the details presented. In order to prevent you from becoming lost or frustrated as you proceed, this chapter will acquaint you with and excite you about nontraditional schools. In an overview, you'll learn:

- The advantages offered by nontraditional schools
- What typical degree programs look like
- Ten innovative ways you can earn credit
- The different types of nontraditional schools

Degrees from Nontraditional Schools Save Money and Time

What is nontraditional education? The term is used in various ways, but a degree program is considered nontraditional if students are not required to sit through classroom instruction to earn most of the credits required for a degree. These students may choose to earn some credits in classroom-based study, but the other types of credit-earning opportunities define the advantages of a nontraditional education.

- Avoid years of study and expense. College credit can be earned for what you already know or intend to learn on your own.
- Create your own program of interesting learning (instead of following a standard degree recipe).
- Accommodate almost any schedule and location.

At a traditional school, you typically complete degree requirements by taking (buying) its courses in its buildings when it chooses to offer them. Also, if you have already learned the material on your own, you probably have to go to all classes anyway. Nontraditional schools are more flexible in the ways you can earn credit; they will grant credit for learning that occurs outside the campus environment.

How much time and money can be saved using nontraditional approaches? Of course, this varies based on individual background, but to illustrate a dramatic advantage, it is possible for a working technical professional with no college credits to earn a bachelor's degree within two years and spend less than $1,000. For some in technical professions, cost is not as much an issue as time. In many cases, students with significant amounts of credit can graduate in less than a year.

As enticing as this sounds, it is wise to consider both the advantages and disadvantages of nontraditional education. Certain aspects of alternative high-tech degrees can be viewed as negative. The pursuit of nontraditional credit requires you to understand degree requirements, initiate your own work, track your progress, and direct school administrators to help you. Within a four-year undergraduate program, a student with poor fundamental college skills (reading, writing, and study habits) can often overcome setbacks with additional help, tutoring, or by choosing less demanding classes. The nontraditional student operates in a more independent fashion, so sound learning skills are required.

There is no guarantee that time and money can be saved at nontraditional schools: convenience has a price in certain situations. Also, if your company, like most technology-oriented companies, has an education reimbursement benefit, check to make sure that it does not exempt certain nontraditional methods (a rare circumstance, however). If there are exemptions, they may not stop you from pursuing a nontraditional degree program, but they will create additional costs. Many of these reimbursement rules are subject to negotiation, and it often pays to challenge them before a higher authority. If you don't know if your company pays for education, find out.

Earn Credit Inside and Outside the Classroom

On the road to a nontraditional high-tech degree, the credits you receive will occur in two areas: credit for what you already know and credit for what you will learn along the way.

Sometimes it's hard to accept that credit is awarded for what you already know. This is an idea you must become comfortable with because it is frequently used in nontraditional programs and is often a large source of credits. Many different methods help schools determine what is college-level learning and how much credit to award. Each nontraditional school tends to favor its own combination of the alternative credit-earning methods, but most schools offer numerous ways to demonstrate knowledge and earn credit. Earning credits for what you already know is akin to taking courses: After a learning process, you will be awarded credit if you can demonstrate competency. In traditional education, you show competency through class attendance, graded assignments, and a final exam. The nontraditional student has many other options, including self-designed learning programs.

Degree Program Requirements

It's important to know specific credit requirements for any nontraditional technical degree program. Requirements for study in core technical areas are understood, but many people are looking for an undergraduate degree without general education/liberal arts credits (graduate degrees are more focused on core study). However, most accredited institutions are committed to rounded education, which includes study outside the intended vocation. It's this aspect that separates colleges from trade and technical schools. The desire for degree programs without liberal arts study may be real, but it is misguided. The argument in favor of degree programs that include liberal arts has been validated by a number of academic studies as well as by the stated requirements of the business community. Imagine a degree that is 100 percent technical education: would graduates gain all the necessary experience in teamwork, team building, historical perspective, and interpersonal communication?

With the recent trend of career-oriented apprenticeship and certificate programs, nontraditional schools are leading the way to recognized degrees with reduced general education requirements. However, liberal arts study is still a near-universal requirement even at nontraditional institutions. Degree programs with both core technical and general education requirements remain the best bet for long-term educational credentials.

Ten Ways to Pick Up More College Credits

Nontraditional credit-building methods are simple to understand, but thorough knowledge of each method will allow you to plan a better credit-building strategy. The basic idea is to use key methods to earn most of your credits. If you have a rough idea of the courses you'll need, you can better determine which methods you'll use.

1. Transfer Credit from Previous College Coursework

If you have completed courses at a college or university, nontraditional schools will accept them for credit, usually with fewer restrictions than traditional schools.

Some credit-building methods (such as independent study) are merely variations on classroom study, while others seem more radical because you design your own coursework and degree program. Identifying the most appropriate credit-building methods can also influence which schools to consider as you build a degree plan (see Chapter 10). The following 10 methods will be described in detail in later chapters.

Typical Degree Credit Requirements

Associate of Science Degree*
   Core technology concentration:

Technical writing	3
Lower-level core study	15
Upper-level core study	15
Liberal arts and sciences:	
Written English	6
Humanities	6
Social sciences	6
Natural science/mathematics	9
Total semester credits	60

Bachelor of Science Degree*
   Core technology concentration:

Technical writing	3
Lower-level core study	27
Upper-level core study	24
Liberal arts and sciences:	
Written English	6
Humanities	9
Social sciences	12
Natural science/mathematics	21
Free electives	18
Total semester credits	120

Master of Science Degree*
   Core technology concentration:

Upper-level preparation	6
Graduate-level core study	24
Graduate thesis/project	8
Total semester credits	38

*This information is meant to convey representative degree requirements. Actual credit requirements will vary from school to school. At each school, specific courses and total credits needed to graduate will vary from degree to degree, depending on the area of study. Many degrees will require more credits to fulfill requirements.

2. Transfer Future College Courses

After selecting your nontraditional school, you can earn credit at almost any accredited school and have the credits transferred when the course is completed.

3. Independent Study

Books and other course materials for self-study are mailed to the student, then he or she returns assignments to the instructor.

These programs are also known as *correspondence courses* and *study-by-mail*.

4. College Course Examinations

Arrangements are made with an accredited institution to take a comprehensive exam for a given course. If the exam is passed, credit for that course is awarded.

5. Standardized Exams

The student takes standardized tests, such as College Level Examination Program (CLEP) and Graduate Record Examination (GRE), at a local testing site. If the scores meet minimum requirements, credit for designated courses is granted.

6. Prior Learning and Portfolio Assessment

The student collects, organizes, and presents information to a nontraditional school describing what has been learned outside the classroom. School personnel evaluate the material and award credits. Experience can be related to work, self-study, hobbies, crafts, volunteering, travel, and most other life experiences.

7. Employee Training/Company-Sponsored Education

Training received as part of a student's employment may be eligible for college credit.

8. Certificates and Licenses

Professional certification exams and licenses usually require tests to be passed. These licenses or certificates can be used to obtain credit for selected courses.

The terms *license* and *certificate* are not synonymous. Licenses are issued by states and indicate that the recipient has completed (among other requirements) the qualifications to practice that occupation or profession by passing a licensing examination and/or meeting with a qualification board.

Certification is usually awarded by a national society, association, or institution of professional practitioners. Certification indicates that a member or candidate for membership has provided evidence of qualification in the field by virtue of a designated number of years of experience served and/or successful passage of an examination developed and monitored by the society, association, or institute. This certification is accepted nationally for a given number of years (usually three) before recertification is necessary.

9. Military Credit

Nontraditional schools routinely evaluate military education, exams, and service ratings to award college credit.

10. Individualized Study

The student defines all or part of the degree program and the manner in which it will be completed. The program is planned in advance with the nontraditional school. Evaluation is required for completeness before credit is given.

An additional consideration when evaluating these methods: Many high-tech engineering degrees (including nontraditional ones) will require coursework in an emerging technology, in which case the standardized exams method would not be suitable (these exams take a long time to create and establish for credit usage). A better choice would be a recently created independent study course.

The Difference Between Matriculation and Enrollment

In this book and most college promotional materials, two words are used frequently in various forms: matriculate and enroll. *Matriculation* means that a student has been accepted by a college or university with the specific intent of completing one of its degree programs. Matriculated students have a commitment from their school that defines, up front, graduation requirements. If the student follows the rules, the school cannot (with rare exceptions) change degree program requirements. The term *enroll* applies to a student who signs up for a college-level course without necessarily having been admitted (matriculated). Nontraditional students matriculate at a single institution but can be enrolled simultaneously in courses at many schools.

How to Choose Between the Two Types of Nontraditional Schools

There are two types of degree-granting nontraditional schools, each appropriate to different situations. To help you decide which is best for you, you must know how they differ from one another.

The first type of nontraditional school doesn't offer courses. It will only evaluate and track your college-level credit-building and award a degree when all requirements are met. For flexibility, this is your best choice. One nontraditional computer software student found that not being tied to a particular college permitted him to move around the country as a contract programmer while making steady progress toward an eventual bachelor's degree. Technology careers can include numerous long-distance moves, so this type of flexibility can be very desirable.

The other type of nontraditional school usually provides a more defined path to follow and is a less extreme departure from traditional degree programs. The following examination of each type of school begins with colleges that not only offer courses, but require them.

Required-Residency Schools

Required-residency schools stipulate that a minimum amount of work must be completed under their auspices. This policy is an attempt to ensure that graduating students will meet a specific school's criteria for graduation. This policy may appear to be an academic pretense for the school's monetary benefit. After all, a student has to pay tuition for each course needed at a required-residency school.

Regardless of the reason for this policy, the minimum amount of required credits is typically equivalent to one traditional year of schoolwork (30 semester hours), and this work will usually be of an advanced (junior or senior) level. While this seems restrictive, keep in mind that many of these schools will allow you to complete all or part of this residency requirement off-campus. A school may offer its own independent study courses, or it may have another alternative that requires only advising sessions (such as individualized study) with a faculty member.

Each school has its own policy, but it boils down to this: When a minimum amount of work is required at a college, you will pay for it at the school's going rate (per credit-hour). How the credit is earned is subject to the offerings and policies of each school. Nontraditional credit-building methods are usually available, and as mentioned before, you may be able to arrange for courses that limit the need to visit the campus. In general, required-residency schools seem to be more well-known and have better reputations than other nontraditional schools.

■■■

Example: Required-Residency Schools

Consider a characteristic, but fictitious, required-residency degree program. Minimum required residency is usually expressed by each school as a certain amount of credit-hours, but for simplicity, number of courses will be used here. Assume you are investigating schools that offer technical management degrees—for example, an MBA with a technology core. Eastern West Virginia State University (EWVSU) has a program consisting of 12 specific courses required to complete its graduate-level engineering/MBA degree. You expect to transfer three courses from previous graduate coursework and challenge two other courses based on prior learning. This totals five courses you expect to get instant credit for, leaving seven to complete. These courses may be completed at remote classrooms, through independent study, or even by using a personal computer and a phone link. However, degree policies require students to complete a minimum of eight EWVSU courses. This means you'll have to take (and pay for) one more course than you'd like.

•••••

In general, if all other things are equal, selecting a school with the least required residency gives you the most flexibility when choosing credit-building methods.

External Schools: No Campus Necessary

At colleges that do not have a minimum residency requirements, it is theoretically possible to matriculate and graduate immediately. All that is required are the college credits to satisfy their degree programs. These institutions can be called *external*. External schools merely store credits earned toward your degree. They may have no involvement in teaching college-level material, although some offer optional courses and exams. Accumulating credits at an external college leads to graduation when you have completed all required work for a degree. You can earn a degree from an external school and never set foot on the campus (if there even is one).

Among nontraditional schools, external colleges have had more success in producing graduates than required-residency schools. The reason is clear: External schools, by definition, have to offer the student more options to earn credit. External schools tend to be more liberal in evaluating various college-level work and accepting it for credit. External degrees are also among the most affordable accredited degrees that can be obtained by individuals experienced in technical fields.

Another option is called a *credit bank*. A credit bank is run by a school as a place where students can temporarily park credits that have been obtained elsewhere. A credit bank does not lead to a degree, but it is useful for undecided or highly mobile students.

At both residency-required and external nontraditional schools, when you satisfy the degree requirements, you graduate.

SUMMARY

By now you should be familiar with some of the fundamental concepts of nontraditional schools, their degree programs, and the credit-earning methods you can use to get the degree you need to meet your goals. The following chapters will teach you when, why, and how you can use alternatives to classroom study to get your degree quicker, more easily, and with less cost.

4

When to Use Traditional Classroom Study

Since this book deals with alternative methods of earning a high-technology degree, it may seem out of place to describe the use of classroom-based study. However, it remains an important credit-building option in even the most radical degree programs, so it must be discussed before nontraditional techniques.

You may remember college course registration as a time of confusing catalogs, long lines, closed courses, last-minute drop-and-add sessions, and, if your school was truly high-tech, numerous keypunch cards you didn't dare fold, spindle, or mutilate. Improvements have been made, so the process is now less frustrating.

To keep updated on courses offered by local colleges and universities, contact each school and have it put you on its regular mailing list. The best place to locate local colleges is in the yellow pages (try the "schools" classification). Many schools will regularly mail their updated course bulletins to the human resource or personnel offices of local companies. If you're willing to commute long distances, most public libraries have handbooks listing all the colleges in the U.S.

Course registration methods differ from school to school; at a particular school, you may get to choose courses from a few methods: wait-in-line, mail-in, call-in, and even automated phone registration. Open registration starts before classes begin; it ends when classes begin or shortly after, giving you the chance to attend the first class and drop it if it doesn't fulfill expectations. Payment in full at registration is still the rule, but the acceptance of credit cards creates a student-controlled form of financial aid.

Class attendance is an important part of traditional classroom study. If you are unfamiliar with the campus, allow yourself extra time before the first class to find parking, the building, and the classroom. Some courses are structured for the benefit of working students: evening classes meeting one or two times a week for two

---

QUICK GUIDE TO CLASSROOM STUDY

Learning centers around regular class attendance. An instructor teaches, gives assignments, and administers tests. Students register for each course before the start of the term. Costs range from hundreds to thousands of dollars for each course. The breadth of classroom course credits available is the standard of comparison for other credit-earning methods described in this book. Typical semester courses earn three or four credits.

Reasons to use: when other methods fall short, networking, prestige, group work/learning with peers

Possible restrictions: prerequisites, cost, treatment not suited to adults

Look for: accreditation, good instructors, prior approval from matriculated school

or three hours, compact four-to-six week courses, and even intensive one- or two-week sessions. Daytime classes for young adults tend toward shorter daily sessions. Courses usually range from eight to twelve weeks long.

At the first class meeting, instructors will discuss what they intend to cover, what methods will be used, what textbooks and other materials will be required, and how students will be graded. In technical courses, laboratory or computer work may be required in addition to assigned reading. The course may have a final exam, but in many technology courses, a project may replace or augment the final.

Students can usually choose from letter grade or pass/fail options at registration. *Pass/fail,* also referred to as *pass/no-pass,* means any grade above a certain level (usually a C or a D) would appear on the transcript as a pass. These grades are not included when computing grade point average (GPA). When given the choice of letter grades or pass/fail, you should consider:

- How well you think you'll do in the course
- How important it is to your degree to do well

This method of selection applies to the other credit-building methods as well.

■■■

Example: Choosing Graded versus Pass/Fail

Suppose the course you're considering is electronics and your degree is electrical engineering. In this case, you should do well and have the grade shown on your transcript. However, if you are considering a course in a long-postponed humanities requirement such as history of western dance, you would be wise to choose the pass/fail option.

·····

FILLED CLASSES

Some traditional classes can fill up fast, and there is no guarantee when they will be offered again. This can be a problem if a specific course is required for your degree. When in doubt, register as soon as possible, and make your final decision about taking the course before the date when you can withdraw and still obtain a full refund.

Schools have the students calculate the tuition costs of courses. They establish a cost per credit-hour, and in the course description they list the number of credits awarded for completion. Costs per credit-hour range from less than $100 at some state-sponsored schools to hundreds of dollars at well-known institutions catering to professionals with corporate tuition reimbursement. Remember, you must pay in advance, and there is no refund if you don't pass. Schools usually publish calendars that establish dates by which you can get all, part, or none of your money back if you choose to withdraw. In addition to the tuition, don't forget miscellaneous registration and student fees, books, childcare expenses, commute costs, and parking fees.

Success in the classroom depends on the motivation. For those with specific degree motivations, high rates of completion and good grades are common. However, previous commitments at work or at home can get in the way. Some students jump in with gusto, sign up for more than one classroom course, and do well; others can barely manage a single evening course every other semester. Because of this, class sizes tend to shrink as courses wind down to completion.

Prerequisites are required for many courses. The idea behind making students complete specific courses in a certain order is to permit the instructors to have an academically prepared class and to throttle the demand for certain key courses. Sometimes there is a thin connection between a course and its listed prerequisite. For instance, many engineering and computer programming courses require completed high-level math courses. In the course, as in the real world, the math used may be limited to a very narrow, practical application. Technical students from the working world have a disdain for this type of restriction. You can look for ways around similar restrictions. One way is to ask the instructor for permission to waive the prerequisite.

Many traditional colleges offer alternatives, such as broadcast courses and accelerated weekend programs, to normal classroom attendance. Ask colleges and universities in your area to identify broadcast alternatives. Also ask about intensive local weekend schools or Program for Adult College Education (PACE) where you can study at home during the week and attend an all-day Saturday session. The end result is that you finish a course with less of the overhead and inconvenience of classroom attendance. Cable television and videotape courses will be discussed in Chapter 6.

Taking college-level courses in the traditional classroom setting has certain advantages, particularly when a nontraditional college requires specific courses that are difficult to complete in other ways. A good example is any course that has a laboratory component (which is difficult, but not impossible, to do with an exam or through the mail). If you decide to matriculate in a residency-required school, you may have to enroll in some of its classroom-based offerings.

You may also choose to participate in classroom study because you want to. It may be the most efficient and enjoyable method

 PASS/FAIL LIMITS

Some schools may limit the number of courses that you can take under pass/fail. Check all degree programs for this type of restriction if you plan on making extensive use of pass/fail. The reason behind this limit is to prevent you from obtaining a straight A average by using the pass/fail option for all but one course.

for certain areas of credit-building. It can also be a way to meet others in your situation and make important career-network connections.

You can make the most of classroom study by finding good teachers and professors. If you have latitude in choosing your classroom study, ask students or the student government to recommend their favorite professors. (Many student governments publish brochures rating professors and classes.) For example, a digital engineer by checking around, ended up enjoying some dreaded coursework required by his degree program.

Major drawbacks to classroom study are cost, completion time, flexibility, and the potential lack of adult treatment. It is possible to find reasonably priced courses, but these tend to be routine, and little accommodation is given to the adult student. At the other end of the spectrum are the accommodating and expensive professional college courses that are usually part of a complete degree program. There's little point in dwelling on these courses because this book primarily deals with other, better opportunities.

∎∎∎

Example: Using the Classroom

A Los Angeles aerospace engineer pursues a master's degree that requires her to complete a course in project management. She finds an evening course offered at a nearby university and discovers the course is taught by an engineering manager from a competing aerospace company. She registers for the three-credit course via phone and pays the $325 tuition using her credit card.

The three-hour class meets once per week; required preparation for each class includes reading two chapters from the textbook as well as article handouts. Progressive project work is assigned and graded throughout the course, and a final exam is given after 12 weeks. The engineer is notified by mail that she has been given an A, after which she can apply for her company's tuition reimbursement.

∙∙∙∙∙

Classroom credits are often applied to degree programs at other schools—that is, you earn the credits at a local college and have them transferred to the school where you've matriculated. Always gain prior approval from your matriculated school for any courses you plan on taking, and always make sure the school is regionally accredited. If you do these two things before registration, transferring the credits to a nontraditional school will go smoothly.

? WHAT IF YOU PREFER CLASSROOM STUDY?

What if you decide that classroom study is the only way for you to learn? Go ahead and use it. This book makes a point of promoting alternative methods and degree programs, but you must find what works for you. If this means grinding it out in classroom-based study, it's still progress. By comparison, credit-building alternatives require more self-motivation, plus a spirit of adventure. For some, these qualities might have been lost to years of educational regimentation.

ACADEMIC ADVISORS

Regarding working with academic advisors to obtain prior approval for credit-earning, a nontraditional graduate looked back on how it helped make for a smooth graduation process:

"There was a lot of touching base with those people (academic advisors) who make decisions and keep you on course, so there wasn't any question of having deviated from the program. There wasn't any doubt about graduation—I met the requirements."

5

Fail-Safe Credit Transfers

Transfer Previously Earned Credits to Your New School

When exploring the method of transfer credit, assume that you have matriculated with a nontraditional school. Of course, you want all the credits you've already earned to transfer. To begin the process of gaining the maximum amount of transfer credit, you need to remember all the institutions from which you've earned college-level credits. Recalling all colleges attended can be a challenge for technical professionals who have lived in many places. It is wise to keep a file that includes all college transcripts. As long as you can remember all the schools you've attended, you can request copies of transcripts and course descriptions from each school. You will want a copy for yourself and one from each school sent to the degree program transcript evaluator at the school with which you've matriculated.

Nontraditional transfer credit evaluators work much like those at traditional schools: They use your college transcripts, associated course descriptions (from college catalogs and bulletins), and reference books that assist in cross-referencing college course offerings. Ultimately, they look for ways to view your old coursework as equivalent credits in the realm of your new school. This initial process can take weeks to accomplish and can go on longer if the transcript evaluator is swamped (as is often the case at certain times during the academic year).

Additional information may be needed about certain courses before you receive correspondence that tells you what courses have been transferred and explains why other courses did not transfer. This is often a form letter with check-off boxes. If you find errors or want to challenge some of the transfer denials, you need to continue the evaluation process. Blatant mistakes or omissions are typically corrected by pointing them out to the transcript evaluator, who will then update the transcript as necessary.

QUICK GUIDE TO CREDIT TRANSFERS

Have your previously completed college credits transferred to the school with which you've matriculated. Transcripts sent from previous schools will be evaluated against the needs of your current degree program. When the evaluation is complete, you will receive a new transcript showing what transferred. Costs for transfer evaluation are minimal at nontraditional schools.

Reasons to use: prevents retaking courses, low cost, easy transfers

Possible restrictions: limits on total transfer credit, aging of courses, unaccredited study, low course grades, recreational courses

Watch for: fickle evaluators, quarter/semester credit conversion

SENDING TRANSCRIPTS

An administrative note: Copies of transcripts you possess are not usually accepted by transcript evaluators. The evaluating school will require transcripts to be sent directly by the school where the course work originated. This is an authenticity measure on the part of the evaluating school, which looks for the postmark, official stationery, and an embossing seal.

CHALLENGING AGE RESTRICTIONS

If you encounter age restrictions for your previously earned credits, use the appeals process. In many cases, technology may be considered to be dated, but isn't in reality. As an example, solid-state electronics have made electron tubes an undeserved symbol of obsolete technology. In fact, tube devices operate using fundamental principles of electronics. Also, when reliable or high-power operation in harsh electromagnetic and radiation conditions is needed, designers still turn to electron tubes for state-of-the-art systems. This reasoning might be used in your time-limitation appeal where the underlying academic principles are as current as the application of that same knowledge. Save your transfer credits any way you can.

When challenging credit transfers, it helps to know the policies schools use when evaluating transcripts. Fortunately, most schools use the same guidelines to develop their policies. Agreement on transferring accredited college credit within the U.S. was formalized in the Joint Statement on Transfer and Award of Academic Credit, which was approved in 1978 and reaffirmed in 1989/90 by the American Council on Education, the American Association of College Registrars and Admissions Officers, the Council on Postsecondary Accreditation (COPA), and the American Association of Community and Junior Colleges.

If you run into any snags in your evaluations, you may find that referring a capricious reviewer to the Joint Statement can save your valuable transfer credits from being thrown away needlessly. Another method to use when you are denied transfer credit is to challenge the denial and provide more backup information: A computer software student who was refused transfer of a FORTRAN course successfully convinced the school's transcript evaluator to reestablish transfer credit by providing her with a copy of the table of contents from the designated course textbook. Other examples of backup information include course syllabi, course notes, or letters from original course instructors or department heads that address the issue of transfer denial.

After completing any work with a transcript evaluator regarding transfer credit, always get an updated transcript. Check this transcript for completeness and accuracy.

What about course grades? Policies vary from school to school, but most fall into two camps: those accepting courses with a D or better, and those accepting courses with a C or better. Of course, transfer students with too many D grades may not meet the minimum grade point average required for matriculation. Students with problems meeting minimum grade point average requirements can ask that certain courses (the ones with low grades) not be transferred in an attempt to raise their overall grade point averages. Portfolio assessment can be a way to get those course credits after matriculation.

A few words on the cost of transfer credit: Most schools evaluate previously earned credits using one of two methods. They either include them in the initial enrollment fee, or they charge on a cost per transfer credit basis. When the enrollment fees cover all credit transfer, you usually get a better bargain if you have much transfer credit to evaluate. Being charged per credit may work out to be cheaper if you have few credits to transfer since you are paying a much lower enrollment fee. In any event, the amount is almost always a small fraction of what it would cost to repeat the courses.

A single rule most influences your success in transferring credit: If you earned credit at a regionally accredited college in the U.S., it will be considered for transfer. A few exceptions and limitations may be encountered, but most students experience no problems transferring this kind of credit to nontraditional schools.

To meet some degree requirements, certain courses must have been taken in recent years to be accepted for credit. This type of restriction is often used to evaluate applied science courses, which are a significant part of most technical degree programs. Where there are maximum age limits for specific courses, the time is usually 10 to 15 years. The reason for this restriction is to produce graduates who have current knowledge in rapidly advancing fields. As an example, a course like classical physics probably will not be subject to age restrictions, but courses in rapidly changing areas such as digital electronics and software might. Age restrictions on coursework should be researched with each school.

Another restriction to be aware of: Some required-residency schools will set a maximum amount of credit you can transfer. Some limit you to 90 semester credits for a bachelor's degree. This limitation does not apply at the external colleges. Also, if the credits you earned are not applicable in some way to the degree requirements, the credits will not be usable. Most degree programs have plenty of free electives into which almost any college course can fit. However, if you use up all your free electives, you may lose some credit transfers. Certain schools will not transfer recreational college courses such as tennis and photography.

Semester/Quarter Credit Hour Systems

Schools who use the quarter calendar and credit system may not see semester credit on old transcripts and, if the mistake is not caught, full credit value is lost. Also, sometimes semester-based schools mistakenly adjust (downward by 33 percent) previous semester credits as if they were quarter-credits.

A short explanation of semester and quarter credit-hour systems should help prevent a loss of credits.

A bachelor's degree requires 120 credits at institutions using the semester system, or 180 credits at institutions using the quarter system. On a calendar, both represent the same amount of effort: four years of full-time study. Why schools use one system or the other isn't important here, but because each semester credit is worth one-and-a-half times as much as each quarter credit, it's vital to make sure this ratio be applied when credit is transferred (see the following table).

TECHNICAL AND TRADE SCHOOL CREDITS

Don't assume that credit received at technical, trade, or other schools lacking regional accreditation will be successfully transferred (although some technical schools do have regional accreditation). While it is possible to pursue evaluation and transfer of nonregionally accredited coursework, the results will vary greatly; much depends on the individual policies of each school. This situation is also addressed in the Joint Statement, which makes no recommendation, but suggests that schools should make an effort to validate such credits. This lack of uniform policy will affect many people who have attended technical schools, including some of the larger, well-known institutes. Accreditation by NATTS (National Association of Technical and Trade Schools) is not regional, but may help students who attempt vocational course transfer. However, the evaluation of these types of credits will be handled with more scrutiny than regionally accredited coursework; there is a tendency to lose credits. It's common for a number of technical institute courses to reduce to a single college course. If the courses you took were not regionally accredited, but were accredited by the National Home Study Council (which has national accreditation that is recognized by COPA), then your chances for transfer credit are increased. Those with unaccredited coursework should not despair because other credit-building methods, especially prior learning, can be used to recapture and legitimize those credits.

?

FOREIGN TRANSCRIPTS

What about credits earned at a school outside the U.S.? The process of credit transfer is somewhat more involved, but not impossible. Within the U.S., there is some uniformity to degree programs, courses, accreditation, and even school calendars. It's this uniformity that is the lever of simplified credit transfers. Talk with a few graduates of foreign schools and you'll realize that those schools can be very different.

A direct approach to foreign credit transfer is to work with the school you have matriculated with. Support your academic advisor with all the information he or she needs to achieve a satisfactory transfer. The problems encountered are usually language differences (on documentation) and proving that the schools attended meet standards set for regionally accredited schools. For some transcript evaluators, all of this can be a daunting first-time experience. Another evaluator at the same school may have more experience in this area, so it may pay to ask for a supervisor's help.

Another approach is to work with a regionally accredited credit bank service. One of the purposes of credit banks is to get uncommon credits onto official transcripts. Credit bank transcript evaluators usually have more experience with foreign transcripts and other hard-to-evaluate coursework. When the evaluation is complete, credits are placed on the credit bank transcript and can be mailed to your degree-granting school for the normal credit transfer process.

continued on next page

Quarter Hour to Semester Hour Conversion

2 quarter hours = 1.3 semester hours

3 quarter hours = 2.0 semester hours

4 quarter hours = 2.6 semester hours

5 quarter hours = 3.3 semester hours

6 quarter hours = 4.0 semester hours

■■■

Example: Credit Transfer

A computer operator who possessed a traditional associate's degree found a nontraditional school offering degrees related to computer technology. After acceptance and enrollment, he worked on transferring credits to this new school. In a short time, he was able to get nearly all of the credits transferred from the school where he earned his associate's degree, as well as 15 other credits taken outside that degree program. Eventually, he matriculated at his new school with 75 of the 120 credits needed to graduate.

•••••

The evaluation of transfer credit is a universal part of any nontraditional degree program, and the liberal acceptance of credit by nontraditional schools is a pleasant surprise to people who have tried and failed to transfer credits from one traditional school to another. The complaint heard most often from students is that traditional colleges and universities are picky and curiously fickle about what credits they accept. Many students have even been left with the impression that the true agenda of traditional transfer-credit evaluations was to throw away as many previously earned credits as possible. A colleague of mine was attempting to transfer some mathematics coursework from an accredited junior college to a traditional state university (where he was matriculated), but his request was denied by the transfer reviewer because the university was very impressed with its own math department. (To be honest, this traditional university was noteworthy for its lack of noteworthiness). However, remember the good news: Nontraditional schools are usually more generous than traditional schools in transfer evaluations.

Making Sure All Your Future Credits Transfer

When students matriculate in a nontraditional school, some credits are usually needed to complete their chosen degree programs. These credits to be earned can be obtained in a variety of ways and can result from enrollment at more than one institution (which is often not the school where the student is matriculated). One important concept needs to be emphasized: Once matriculated in degree programs, nontraditional students can earn credit by using (depending on their preferences) any combination of credit-building methods from any combination of institutions. This means that the typical student, in addition to earning needed credits, will be engaged in ongoing credit transfers during the degree-completion process. Understanding how to transfer previously earned college credits is the basis of successfully transferring credits yet to be earned. However, for future credits, the process is used for smaller, incremental evaluation of very recent credit awards. The intent is still to get those transcripts to the degree-granting school. The transcript evaluator will then use the transcripts to determine whether to transfer credit.

Apply the same guidelines as with previously earned credit transfers (although course age is not an issue here). An additional precaution: Get approval in advance, preferably in writing and on the school's letterhead, from your academic advisor. This is a confirmation that each credit-building method and course you select will satisfy a particular degree requirement. Without prior approval, you risk wasting time, effort, and money on credits that won't further the degree process.

Some approvals are simple for advisers: For example, needing linear algebra credits, you decide to use a regionally accredited independent study course called MTH 134—Linear Algebra. This is straightforward, so a telephone commitment from your advisor may suffice. Other methods may be more complex for advisors to evaluate, so allow enough time for approval, and aim to get it before any registration deadlines.

Consider this situation: You enroll at a school so you can use a particular credit-building method (for example, portfolio assessment) and then have that credit transferred to the school with which you've matriculated. This is legitimate, but make sure that the school with which you've matriculated will accept credit transfers for that particular credit-building method (some schools will not accept certain types of credit transfers).

What if you matriculate in a nontraditional school and already have all the credits needed to graduate? Great!

continued from previous page

If you can find a faculty member at the school you matriculate with who is from the country where your foreign credits were earned, either you or the transcript evaluator should bring this person into the process to help translate coursework into a local equivalent.

Also, schools can engage the services of independent foreign transcript evaluators. Colleges and universities often prefer to work with agencies of their choice, but if you encounter trouble getting foreign credit transferred, make sure your school has considered this option.

Most importantly, choose the method that is going to yield the most complete transfer of foreign credits.

QUICK GUIDE TO FUTURE CREDIT TRANSFERS

To complete a nontraditional degree, transferring credits from sources outside your degree-granting school gives you more flexibility in earning credits, and encompasses all the credit-earning methods described in this book. Ease of transfer depends on accreditation and applicability to a degree program. As with previously earned transfer credit, a successful evaluation of transcripts leads to the awarding of credit. Costs for ongoing evaluation are minimal.

Reasons to use: applies to most credit-building methods

Possible restrictions: total transfer limit, colleges that offer all coursework for their own degrees

Watch for: proper accreditation, advanced approval

6

Independent Study Courses as Close as Your Own Mailbox

The nontradtional degree method known as *independent study* (also called *correspondence instruction* and *study-by-mail*) is so-named because it describes both the method of learning and the type of temperament required by the student.

To take independent study courses from an institution that offers them, no matriculation is required—you just sign up for the courses. If there are suggested prerequisites for a course, you can go ahead and sign up even if you have not completed, or never intend to complete, those prerequisites. Some schools offering independent study also have their own non-traditional external degree programs. To get an idea of what courses are available, check in the career section at a public library for directories that catalog independent study courses available across the U.S. Individual schools offering independent study will, at your request, send detailed independent study catalogs. These are more detailed than typical college catalogs. Enrolling in an independent study course can be accomplished by mail, phone, or fax; credit cards are usually accepted.

When you enroll in an independent study course, you receive by mail all study materials, including a course outline or syllabus, notes from the instructor, textbooks (if ordered with the course), assignments, and college policies pertaining to independent study. It is then up to you to follow the course instructions and return the assignments to the professor for grading. There are usually five to fifteen assignments, with each graded assignment sent back to you. Every school has a different policy, but you are usually encouraged to complete one assignment and move onto the next lesson while waiting for the previous results to be returned. Some schools permit you to send in two assignments at once. The time it takes to get graded assignments back can range from two to three weeks, but it can take longer for numerous reasons, including busy teachers (many are working professionals) and administrative delays. You should know what the maximum assignment grading

QUICK GUIDE TO INDEPENDENT STUDY

Using course materials delivered to you by mail (and other remote methods such as video), you study and complete assignments at your own pace, without face-to-face instruction. A proctored final exam may be required at the end of regular study. Costs vary, but are a notch higher than traditional classroom study, ranging from low- to mid-hundreds of dollars.

Reasons to use: accommodates mobility and busy schedules, self-paced, easy enrollment, large selection of courses

Possible restrictions: requires self-motivation, shortage of lab courses, costs are similar to or higher than traditional methods, special equipment needed

Look for: quality VCR/cable based off-campus study

times are and hold the school to those times; keeping a log of when each assignment is sent helps track progress. Notify the independent study office if your assignments don't come back on time.

After you complete the last assignment, an exam is usually required. This exam may be given at a location near you, subject to the restrictions of the school and professor. If you can arrange it, traveling to a designated testing site (the school itself, or a branch office of the school) is usually the least complicated and cheapest alternative. If travel is out of the question, you must arrange to have the exam proctored locally.

Whatever arrangements you make to take an independent study final exam, you'll probably be the only person taking the exam. The exam is mailed in advance to your designated proctor. On exam day, that proctor follows the written instructions, which are contained in a sealed envelope, for giving you the test materials. For many students, this test environment has a lower anxiety level than traditional exams, which may lead to higher scores. After you complete the exam (or when time runs out), the proctor takes the exam papers and mails them in for grading.

The exam is graded by the teacher, the final course grade is computed, and a course completion certificate is mailed to you. A transcript may then be sent (by the college that offered the independent study) to the college where you are matriculated which allows credit to be applied to your nontraditional degree program. If the college giving the independent study course is the same as the matriculated college, no transfer is necessary.

A majority of independent study courses are offered as an outreach of traditional schools. The cost of an independent study course is somewhat higher than the cost of taking the same course in a classroom. There also may be a premium charged for newer (such as video) course delivery systems. When calculating total costs, don't forget to include the costs of textbooks, proctors, phone calls to the instructor, and mailing costs of assignments.

Independent study instructors often see a fair amount of dropouts, but students who finish usually get high grades. The problem for dropouts is usually not the course, but instead the absence of external motivation, which is required by this type of coursework. When a student has the proper motivation to finish one independent study course, he or she typically completes all required courses.

Schools offering independent study usually set a minimum completion time (often on the order of four months), but not many students can complete courses that quickly since grading and processing assignments can outpace even the fastest students.

PROCTORS

You should consider two issues regarding proctors: finding one and determining what fee you will need to pay. You may use proctors with whom you can make no-cost or low-cost arrangements. Some examples of these are professors or test officers at a local college, high school principals, public librarians, notary publics, and certified public accountants. The more you plan to use independent study, the harder you should look for an inexpensive, stable proctor.

You must arrange to use a proctor with the approval of the school in which you are enrolled. Typically, this is done by indicating on a form (sent in with the last assignment) who the proctor is and what his or her qualifications are. This form also tells the school where to send the exam.

The keys to successfully completing independent study courses are good reading and writing skills and having the discipline to complete readings and assignments.

Sample of Independent Study Course Costs

Course (School, Department, Semester Credits)	Tuition*	Text
Digital Integrated Circuit/Logic Design (University of California, Engineering, 3)	$310	$67
Fracture Mechanics** (University of Idaho, Mechanical Engineering, 3)	$726	$86
Foundations of Digital Computing (Indiana University, Computer Science, 3)	$213	$76

*Costs illustrate the relative differences at the date of this book's publication. Tuition and other educational costs tend to change rapidly.
**Video course at the master's degree level

Independent study is also administered through Defense Activity for Non-Traditional Education Support (DANTES). Most colleges offering independent study also participate in this military-based program. Using DANTES may prove more convenient than finding your own proctor. Veterans and active military personnel may also be eligible for financial assistance. Further information about DANTES and financial aid can be obtained through a local military affairs branch, the testing office at a local college, or a federal/state Veterans Administration office.

New Methods of Independent Study

Independent study is growing up because of its increasing use of lab materials, broadcast and cable television, video tapes, on-line classes, and transmission of assignments via computer and modem connections.

In general, video courses are still a maturing educational method. The quality of lectures and presentations varies widely. Some of the best are produced by commercial companies; the worst tend to come from colleges and universities—something about being taped for video can turn a normally dull professor into a prescription-quality sleeping aid. Complaints about video courses are common, so if you consider using video-based coursework, be careful. Reviewing a sample of the presentation is reasonable, and most institutions will comply with this request. Also, inspect associated course materials beforehand. The VCR is a useful tool for students in the video classroom: Instruction can be started, interrupted, repeated, and stopped at will.

To get an idea of what video courses are like, make a quick check of your local television listings for telecourses. The largest educational cable network, Mind Extension University (ME/U), is carried by many cable systems. ME/U offers accredited undergraduate and graduate college courses that represent the future of video education: better quality, more course offerings, and affiliations with respected traditional institutions for degree programs that can be completed entirely outside the traditional classroom.

University of Phoenix Online in San Francisco offers on-line classes as part of its graduate degree programs in business and management. In addition to text readings, classes are conducted with students using their personal computers and modems as part of an electronic classroom. Students are instructed, of course, but other communication occurs using the link: conferences with the instructor, group projects, and study sessions among students.

Video training and on-line courses are only alternate methods of course delivery. They both include qualities of correspondence self-study: They require self-discipline to complete, and the quality of the courses varies. The quality of video teaching is generally inferior (from an educational standpoint) to the textbook and syllabus methods. However, new methods such as video are still evolving and will improve in the future.

Other Aspects of Independent Study

Among the nontraditional methods, independent study is usually the most straightforward way to earn credit for what you know or would like to learn. The chief advantage of independent study if you are pursuing a high-tech career is the convenience of working at your own pace at home or on the road. You can schedule your completion around an active or unpredictable career that includes travel, job transfers, and even major life disruptions like becoming a parent. Enrolling in independent study is almost as convenient as ordering a pizza.

Even though you may never meet your independent study instructor face-to-face, it's usually a good idea to establish contact. If an assignment is returned with a less-than-satisfying grade, you could write or phone the instructor and ask how to improve that grade. If the final exam is new, a phone call about what's expected will give you a good idea of what you need to study. It's common for the independent study professor to be the author of the course. Find some way to connect with the instructor—it's like long-distance apple polishing.

Independent study enrollment is open to nearly everyone, and there are many sources of information pertaining to technical subjects as well as a number of other courses that can help complete general education credits. Over 70 regionally accredited college and universities offer over 5,000 independent study courses at the undergraduate and graduate levels. However, there is presently a shortage of courses that incorporate laboratory-type work.

For some, independent study is a way to add technically impressive colleges and universities to job applications and résumés such as the University of Michigan, the New York Institute of Technology, and Brigham Young University, to name just a few.

■■■

Example: Using Independent Study

Independent study can also be used for courses related to computers and programming. One nontraditional student was relying primarily on credit-building techniques, but found the degree program wouldn't be complete without required courses (nine total credits) in database systems, structured programming, and systems analysis. For time reasons, this student found she preferred to obtain these credits through various colleges via independent study. Finding the proper internal motivation was difficult during her first course, so she needed a time extension for completion. After that, pacing became easier, and ultimately she had to put pressure on the database instructor to keep up with grading assignments.

•••••

The disadvantages of independent study are not so obvious. As mentioned earlier, it requires a good deal of self-motivation to complete. A person who can complete studies in this fashion is demonstrating autonomy beyond that of the classroom student. There are usually minimum and maximum time limits for completion, and for those without self-motivation, the maximum completion time can arrive very quickly. Another disadvantage is that these courses can take more time than classroom study. When used as the primary credit-building method, graduation by the independent study method will tend to occur later. It's not, however, the slowest method. Independent study can also be more expensive than classroom-based study. The time delay between

---

SELF-MOTIVATION

Regarding the differences between classroom and independent study, one graduate says,

"In a traditional school, you sign up, sit in a class, do what you're told, sign up again, sit in a class, do what you're told...with this (independent study) you are self-directed and self-motivated. You get some guidance, but what you are working with is primarily your own determination."

assignments and grades requires some personal adjustment. Still, plenty of students love independent study so much that they hate to go back to the classroom to earn credits.

You can expect accredited independent study credits to transfer as easily as similar credits earned in the classroom. Directories of schools offering independent study can be found at most college or public libraries. A directory (or any other regularly updated catalog) is a good starting point for finding course offerings. Again, look for regional accreditation at each institution offering courses that interest you.

7

Cut Your Degree Completion Time with Exams

Using Challenge Examinations for Course Credit

Challenge exams and standardized exams are the two main ways to earn credit through routine testing. Each has different characteristics, but they both have the potential of earning significant amounts of college credits. As you read through this chapter, note which tests seem to be of interest to you.

College students often hear what they think is a rumor or folk story that says, "If you can take and pass the final exam in engineering drawing, you don't have to go to any of the classes!" This is far from a rumor, because you can earn credit in hundreds of college courses by passing comprehensive exams.

Students who want to use this method must first identify examination sources. Course credit by examination is offered by about 25 percent of the colleges and universities that offer independent study. To fully investigate all available course exams, start with a comprehensive independent study guide/catalog that identifies schools offering credit by exam, then obtain catalogs from each school of interest. At local traditional schools, a moderate amount of detective work may uncover some surprising waiver or departmental exam offerings.

After finding appropriate course examinations, the second step in using this method is to gain the advance approval of the nontraditional school where you are matriculated. As with all other credit-building methods, the degree-offering college is not necessarily the same as the school that offers course-credit examinations. When getting approval from your school, specify which degree requirement(s) you are trying to meet through exam challenges. After you have approval, register for the course exam directly through the offering institution.

QUICK GUIDE TO CHALLENGE EXAMINATIONS

You earn credit by passing exams that comprehensively test knowledge gained in equivalent college courses. After registering for an exam, you prepare to take it by using a syllabus or content breakdown. After scheduling and taking the exam, you have passing grades sent to your degree-granting school. Costs range from 25 to a few hundred dollars. Exams are available in many individual liberal art and technical course areas. Typically, three to six credits are awarded.

Reasons to use: establishes individual course knowledge, no homework/assignments

Possible restrictions: requires self-motivation, costs are equal to or higher than traditional methods

Look for: advance approval for all exams

In order to pass the final exam, you have to know the material. Upon registration for credit by examination, you are given the course outline, a list of recommended textbooks, and other materials to aid your study. Again, preparation for the test is almost entirely up to the student (although some schools have advisors available). Beginning at registration, a deadline may be set for taking the exam (you schedule the exam when you're ready). After you take the exam, it's graded and the results are sent to you. Unlike typical final exams, the graded exam is not sent to the student for inspection. If you have a passing score, you arrange to have the result passed on to your degree-granting school. Policies on retaking exams vary, but this credit-earning method tends to limit the number of attempts you have to pass.

Actual exam makeup varies from course to course but can include multiple-choice, short-answer, and short-essay questions. The exams are comprehensive tests of what is taught in individual college courses. (It is not realistic to expect, as in some traditional final exams, that you can get by answering a few questions at length.) At some schools, in addition to exams, completed reports or a thesis may be required to earn credit. Many nontraditional institutions have specifically developed all-out credit-by-examination programs. In most of these programs, students may register at distant schools for credit by examination and arrange to have the exam proctored locally (in the same manner as proctored independent study examinations). Some traditional institutions have developed waiver exams as an unpromoted, secondary way of completing coursework.

If you're a technical professional who already knows course material, this method can be a quick, objective way to pick up specific course credits. If you intend to learn course material on your own, this credit-building method is similar to independent study, but without assignments and the associated feedback on progress.

A disadvantage of this method is that you might have to pay both your degree-granting school and the school that offers the challenge exam (unless these schools are the same). In certain cases, the total cost may be less than it would be for actually taking one comparable course, but in general, this method usually isn't the least expensive way to earn credit. Also, as with independent study, the student must rely almost entirely on internal motivation to be successful.

The difference between this credit-building method and standardized tests (detailed in the next section) is fuzzy. The following

✓ LOOKING AT A GRADED EXAM

Some schools can make arrangements for you to review your exam results. One method is to travel to the campus and, under supervision, look over the graded paper. Since this is not practical for students enrolled at a distance, arrangements can often be made to phone the instructor and discuss the exam results.

examples characterizing two of the largest programs developed to gauge typical single-course learning through one exam will help clarify the differences between the two methods.

■ ■ ■

Example: Course Exam Programs

Ohio University (OU) Examinations is an examination program with almost 200 course exams (many of which can apply to technical degree programs) such as digital electronics, industrial engineering drawing, computer science, chemical engineering, and a full range of scientific and math course equivalents. Students who enroll in OU Examinations are given brief syllabi, lists of study materials, and descriptions of the examination itself. Each supervised examination must be taken within six months of enrollment. Scheduling the exam and any other needed preparation is left to the student. Credit from OU is given in quarter units, so students must watch these credits when transferring to schools that use the semester credit system. The cost per exam attempt is about $100.

Thomas Edison College Examination Program (TECEP) is another source of undergraduate course credit by examination, with a few exams in the realm of computer programming, database, and applications. Though the TECEP exams are affiliated with Thomas Edison College, they are accepted at many other institutions as well. These tests were prepared by teams of college faculty who have taught comparable courses. Each TECEP ex-amination is based on an outline of a particular area of study and is mostly made up of multiple-choice questions (although some include short-answer or essay questions). In the event of test failure, TECEP exams can be retaken only once. These exams are inexpensive: $35 per attempt (less for New Jersey residents), which is less than $12 per credit hour. A comprehensive description of all TECEP exams is published yearly by Thomas Edison State College. It can be purchased for $10 from their registrar's office.

See App. B for addresses of and more information about OU and TECEP.

• • • • •

If challenge examinations appeal to you, consider during your search for a degree-granting institution that not all schools will accept these credits. A few schools, including some nontraditional ones, will not permit these credits to easily transfer; many schools make a point of indicating in their academic policies which course-examination programs they will accept results from.

QUICK GUIDE TO STANDARDIZED EXAMINATIONS

Blocks of credit are granted when passing scores are made on standardized tests (like CLEP). You register for the exams and have the scores sent to your degree-granting school. Examination costs are typically less than $100, and large blocks of credit are granted in various academic areas and technical disciplines.

Reasons to use: large blocks of credit, usually inexpensive, objective pass/fail scoring, no penalty for not passing, excellent for general education/liberal arts

Possible restrictions: all degree programs accept different exams, limited amount of technical exams and graduate-level credit

Look for: applicability to degree programs, advance registration dates for each exam

1. Orson Welles' *Citizen Kane* was significant for its
   a. complex narrative structure
   b. subtle film techniques
   c. portrayal of a simple assuming man
   d. emphasis on flat, even lighting

2. The New German cinema, including films by Wim Wenders and Rainer Fassbinder
   a. was sentimental and superficial in comparison with Italian Neo-Realism and the French New Wave
   b. had limited commercial success in the U.S., in part due to the decline of art movies theaters
   c. ignored American film genres in the attempt to define a common European cinematic language
   d. rejected earlier German film tradition established by Fritz Lang and F.W. Murnau

3. Buster Keaton is known for
   a. spectacular physical skills
   b. being a "ladykiller"
   c. sentimental comedy
   d. witty repartee

Sample Questions from TECEP Examination
Introduction to the History of Film

Reprinted with permission from Thomas Edison State College, *Test Descriptions* © 1991.

6. The division of the nervous system which is concerned with "fight or flight" is
   a. central
   b. parasympathetic
   c. peripheral
   d. sympathetic

7. The Organ of Corti is found in the
   a. outer ear
   b. inner ear
   c. Eustachian tube
   d. middle ear

8. The blood vessels having the most elastic tissue are
   a. capillaries
   b. veins
   c. lymphatics
   d. arteries

Sample Questions from TECEP Examination
Anatomy and Physiology

Reprinted with permission from Thomas Edison State College, *Test Descriptions* © 1991.

SPECIAL EXAM ARRANGEMENTS

Most standardized exams are given at regularly scheduled periods throughout the year at high schools, colleges, and universities. In special cases, local exams can be arranged at an open site close to you.

Earn Large Blocks of Credit Through Standardized Exams

Since the mid-'50s, most high school graduates have been exposed to standardized tests, usually culminating in the Scholastic Achievement Test (SAT). Nontraditional college students can use college-level standardized tests to earn credit in a wide array of subjects. Many of these exams were intended for other evaluation purposes, but years of college work in engineering, computers, science, and liberal arts can be credited at a cost-per-credit-hour rate not seen in decades.

The process of using standardized tests to earn credit is direct. By knowing which exams your school accepts and what courses you need to complete, you can search for tests to take. To illustrate, if you need to earn six credits in lower-level college mathematics and your school will accept CLEP exams, you might consider one of the three algebra and trigonometry CLEP exams.

You must also understand how your school will award credit for each exam—how many credit hours you'll receive and in what subject area. (This is usually covered in the college catalog or bulletin.) To continue with the previous example, the CLEP exam in college algebra is worth three credits at your degree-granting school, so to satisfy the six credits you might also consider taking the CLEP trigonometry test.

Information on specific exams is available from your nontraditional school. A quick way to get exam bulletins/programs and registration sheets is to visit the testing office at a local college. As a last resort, contact individual testing services by phone or mail; they will send out complete information on the tests, including where and when each exam will be given.

After reviewing the test descriptions and selecting which exams to take, you should double-check with your academic advisor before exam registration to make sure selected exams can be used to satisfy your degree program's credit requirement. A careful understanding of applicability is important; always get advance approval, and be careful that each exam will be awarded credit for your specific degree requirements. A college might not accept approved examinations for all degree programs. For example, a school might grant credit when the CLEP subject exam is information systems if it is meant to be applied to an information science degree, but the school may choose to not grant credit when the intent is to apply it toward an engineering-oriented computer science degree.

To register, you fill out a form with your name, address, exam titles, preferred exam dates (chosen from the available dates), where scores should be mailed, and other information. When you send in the registration form with the test fee (which varies with

 REGISTRATION DEADLINES

Be aware: There are deadlines for registration, sometimes months before the exam date. If you miss the deadline, sometimes you can pay a late fee to register (if you are in time for the second deadline). If you miss all deadlines, at some exams you can show up at the test site with a completed registration and a check/money order to try to take the exam as a standby (if there are enough seats and an available exam).

exam) you will receive an admission ticket; this ensures that your exam and a seat will be reserved at the test site.

When exam day arrives, you will find the environment very structured. Various security measures are taken to make sure the right person is taking the test (a photo ID is a common requirement). You should read, in advance, the test rules that accompany the admission ticket. Knowing these rules, concerning areas such as calculator usage, are part of being exam-ready. Exam instructions are read aloud from a script to all test-takers. In most cases, each exam and portions of exams are timed. Standardized exams are often the familiar "fill in the circle with a no. 2 pencil." Some exams use short answer or essay questions.

When the test is complete, the exams are collected and sent in to be scored. Most exams are designed to be scored by computer, although tests with written or oral components are scored by human evaluators. Scores are returned in four to six weeks and are mailed to students and to the schools designated (by the test-taker) to receive them.

These exams are professionally prepared in an attempt to have the exam results conform to a normal distribution—that is, all scores from low to high follow a bell-shaped curve. With standardized exams (more than with other credit-building methods), your level of preparation determines how well you can do.

If you don't pass, you have a few options. You can retake the exam with no penalty (other than having to pay again). With some exams, you can pay for a graded copy so mistakes can be analyzed to prepare for the next attempt. However, if you take an exam more than once, there is little chance you'll see the same questions again, much less the same exam. After you receive your scores, if you think a mistake has been made in grading, you can request that your test be hand-scored for an additional charge.

Per-exam fees are usually under $100, but if you are using these exams to establish credit in areas in which you are learning, you should consider the costs of study materials as part of the overall cost.

Which tests are accepted and how much credit they are worth depends on the policy of the college where the student is matriculated. For instance, most schools will accept the AP and CLEP exams, but only a handful will accept the GRE subject exam for credit. Each school will establish its own minimum passing scores. When you consider that most nontraditional schools will let you

? GOING DOWN IN STYLE

Suppose you know the exam is going badly, and you have no chance of getting a passing score. What can you do? When you are sure this is true and not just normal testing anxiety, you should adopt a new strategy. During many exams, you can bail out by filling in a box on the answer sheet that indicates, "Never mind, don't bother scoring, and make no record or report about this test." If you choose to do this, you can spend the rest of the time going over the test to learn about it as part of the preparation for your next attempt.

take a test over and over without penalty until it is passed, you may wonder, "What's the catch?"

When you consider any standardized exam, it's helpful to use one of three approaches.

1. You already know the material covered in an exam and are ready to take it.
2. You are familiar with the material, but need some review before taking the exam.
3. The material covered in the exam will form the basis for studying an unfamiliar subject. You will take the exam only when you feel you're fully prepared.

All these approaches share the same goal: earning college credit. In the first two approaches, the exams are used to validate existing knowledge; in the third approach, the method resembles independent study and course examination. Familiarize yourself with the exam content and determine which approach you should use. This way, you can get a feel for how much effort will be required to earn credit.

Many nontraditional students set up a study strategy for exams where they prepare only to pass the exam, not to get the best score possible. In this situation, a technology student might choose to use a GRE engineering or GRE computer science exam (or both) and then study, in-depth, about half of the topics covered in that exam. If this amount of studying is enough to get a passing score, this is a legitimate strategy for those primarily interested in credit, but it's not necessarily a broad educational experience.

Some claim that an ability to be test wise can be developed for certain standardized exams. A word of warning: Standardized exams are engineered to eliminate luck as a factor. There is no substitute for knowing the material an exam is meant to test. Students often develop testing strategies through the use of various exam-taking techniques that may enhance the chances of receiving the desired score.

For instance, a common method used on fill-in-the-circle exams is to mark answers in the question booklet, then go back near the end of the exam period to transfer answers to the answer sheet. The premise is that the test-taker stays focused on the questions, and there's less chance to make errors filling out the answer sheet. Exam strategies like this can be found in a variety of books related to exam-taking, but they are usually not in the officially endorsed study guides published under the auspices of the institution creating the exams.

A potential disadvantage to this method is that some students do worse than others when taking standardized exams. Plus, when

YOU DON'T HAVE TO BE THE BEST

Here's another plus for aggressive credit-builders using these tests: Top scores are not necessary to pass. In some cases, 40th-percentile scores can earn a block of credit equal to one year of full-time study.

you consider the pass/fail system, there are two sides: Passing is a great relief and its own reward, but failing (especially after a period of extended study) can be discouraging.

It's a legitimate nontraditional credit-building technique to take the exam until you pass. Two suggestions if you this approach: It could take more than few tries, and you shouldn't quit studying until scores come back that confirm your success. Always reregister right after taking the exam if you aren't 100 percent confident you passed.

YOUR NAME

First 6 Letters of Last Name

YOUR NAME: _____ (PRINT)   Last Name   First Name   M.I

MAILING ADDRESS: _____ (PRINT)   P.O. Box or Street Address

City   State   Country   Zip or Postal Code

CENTER: _____ (PRINT)   City   State   Country

Use only a pencil with a soft, black lead (No. 2 or HB) to complete this answer sheet. Be sure to fill in completely the space that corresponds to your answer choice. Completely erase any errors or stray marks.

DATE OF BIRTH   **SEX** ○ Male   ○ Female

Month   Day   **REGISTRATION NUMBER**   **TITLE CODE**

Typical Multiple-Choice Standardized Test Scoring Sheet

Computer-based tests are a new alternative to weeks of waiting and worrying following an exam. These pencil-free exams are now offered in many subject areas and have two main benefits: instant score reporting and a much larger selection of testing days. For example, the usual GRE exams are given five times a year, but if you choose to take a computerized test, arrangements can be made to take it any Monday, Wednesday, or Friday (ETS has contracted with 130 Sylvan Learning Centers throughout the country to administer this option). To explore this option, contact each testing service directly.

Members of the armed forces can arrange to take many standardized tests on base at a reduced charge (arrange through DANTES by contacting the base education office). If you live far from an official test site, you may be able to arrange for an examination at a closer location; review individual exam bulletins for specific information.

Skip One Year of College with Five CLEP Exams

College Level Examination Program (CLEP) tests are regularly used to earn credit by degree-seeking students (including traditional ones) to save time and money. Over 4 million people have taken CLEP tests. Among all credit-earning standardized tests, CLEP tests are the most widely accepted by colleges and universities. If you consider standardized exams, look first at the CLEP exams to bypass course requirements. There are two types of CLEP tests: general and subject exams.

The five CLEP general exams in English composition, mathematics, humanities, natural science, and social science/history are a quick way to complete one year's worth of a degree's general education requirement. The total cost: $200 and an afternoon. The CLEP general exams are important because most degree programs have general education requirements that these CLEP exams begin to satisfy. The English general exam not only earns six semester credits, but also may satisfy the requirement to pass a college-level writing course (written English is a mandatory requirement at nearly every accredited college in the U.S.). If the English composition exam doesn't satisfy the English requirement, the English Composition with Essay CLEP exam usually will.

There are more than 30 CLEP subject exams in business, science, mathematics, history, foreign languages, and composition/literature; each is equivalent to typical college courses. When you use CLEP subject exams as an alternative to challenge exams, you'll probably save money and time. While there are currently few

 CLEP PUBLICATIONS

If you're contemplating taking CLEP tests, take a look at *The Official Handbook for the CLEP Examinations.* It contains descriptions of all CLEP exams, sample questions and answers for each exam, and includes a definitive guide to preparing for exams with lists of reference materials. If you can't find it at your library, look for the earlier edition, *The College Board Guide to the CLEP Examinations.*

exams related directly to technology, the science and math exams can be used along with other liberal arts exams to satisfy general degree requirements. One near-technical exam involves information systems and computer applications, which may satisfy lower-level computer software or applied science degree requirements.

The CLEP general exams test knowledge similar to that of a better high-school education. They are frequently administered to incoming college freshmen. Each general CLEP test may be worth six semester credits. The CLEP subject exams are built around the contents of standard college courses (American history, 1865 to present, for example), and students with some general knowledge can prepare for the exams using study guides. The usual award for subject exams is three to six credits.

All CLEP exams are administered frequently during the year at most major colleges. These exams are all the familiar multiple-choice, fill-in-the-bubble type, although some have written response sections. The exams cost less than $40 each, but certain sites add a small fee for administering the 90-minute tests.

Useful test guides for all CLEP exams abound in libraries and bookstores. Most exam guides contain sample questions, exam content breakdown (by subject area), and the names of textbooks that will help you prepare for each subject exam.

■■■

Example: Engineer Uses CLEP

A Silicon Valley computer engineer who matriculated in a bachelor-level technology degree needed nine general education credits to complete a liberal arts requirement. Investing $13 in various used texts about art history and American history, he studied for a month and a half in preparation for the subject exam American history II (1865 to the present) and the general humanities exam. The exams were administered at a nearby college. Results arrived a month later that showed he had scored in the 90th percentile for American history and in the 80th percentile in humanities. These were well beyond the minimum scores needed and he was awarded nine credits; total costs came to about $100. He notes, "Even though I've never had a class in humanities, as an adult I've read about the arts and their history in order to appreciate trips to museums, concerts, and literature. I chose the second American history exam because it was still familiar from high school and, as strange as it sounds, a significant portion of the exam's questions concerned events that happened within my lifetime."

.....

If you cannot obtain a test schedule or registration forms from the testing office at a local college, contact CLEP directly.

College Level Examination Program (CLEP)
P.O. Box 6600
Princeton, NJ 08541-6600
(609) 951-1026

12. The IF-THEN construct in computer programming is diagrammed by which of the following?

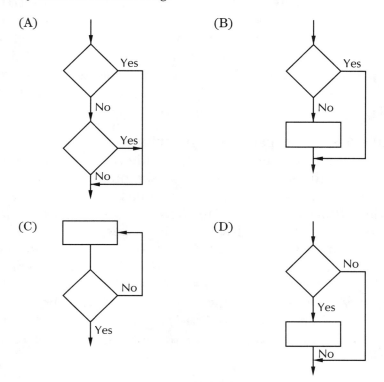

(E) None of the above

13. The process of finding incorrect operation in a computer program is called

(A) iteration   (B) debugging   (C) specification
(D) testing   (E) recursion

Questions in the Style of CLEP Subject Examination
Computers and Data Processing

Use AP Exams to Bypass College Courses

In the acclaimed movie *Stand and Deliver*, a Los Angeles high school math teacher motivates underprivileged students to earn college credit through the Advanced Placement (AP) Program mathematics exam. Every year, more than 200,000 high school students take AP exams to enter college with advanced standings. Bypassing the entire first year of college is common. Although these exams are typically administered to high school seniors,

AP SCORES AND CREDIT AWARDS

AP exam scores range from one to five; scores of three, four, or five are usually considered passing. The AP Program estimates that 67 percent of AP test-takers score three or better. Some colleges choose to scale the credit awarded up or down based on the actual AP exam score obtained.

adult nontraditional college students can take them to meet many general education requirements, and some degree-specific ones as well. Exams are given in these technical and scientific areas: calculus, computer science, biology, chemistry, and physics. Other AP test areas are music, art, history of art, English, American history, Latin, French, German, and Spanish. At nontraditional schools, AP exams are almost as widely accepted as CLEP exams.

You should exercise more care in planning for AP exams because the tests are administered only once a year (in the spring). To take an AP exam, you have to locate a high school participating in the AP Program and register through it. When you contact high schools, they may be surprised that an adult wants to register, and they may explain that AP is only for high school students. This is wrong; you should insist upon registering. If the search for a participating school goes slowly, contact the AP Program for help.

High school students participate in multiple-year AP courses. To help the students and their teachers, a wide variety of educational material from the AP Program exists: sample exams, course descriptions, free-response grading examples, and general testing strategies. While it is usually not feasible for the nontraditional student to attend these high school AP classes, these preparation materials can help anyone prepare for the exams. The materials are easy to order, but it may also be possible to borrow them at no cost from a local high school AP teacher. Like CLEP, commercial study guides for AP exams are also available in libraries and bookstores. The AP Program publishes the *Guide to the Advanced Placement Program* and the *Bulletin for Students*; both are free upon request from AP.

The AP exams are similar to CLEP exams, although they have free-response essay sections in addition to multiple-choice questions. Most of the examinations last three hours; results can take more than six weeks to receive. The credit awarded varies depending on the exam taken and the school where you are matriculated, but most exams are worth six to eight college semester credits.

Each test costs approximately $75, so assuming a typical award of six credits, the cost per credit hour is just over $12.

Another reason to take the AP exam is as a warm-up for a GRE exam (which is described later). The AP exam's content corresponds to lower-level portions of the GRE; the test results of the AP exam may indicate how well prepared the student is for the GRE.

Advanced Placement (AP) Program
P.O. Box 6670
Princeton, NJ 08541-6670
(609) 771-7300

USING THE AP EXAM

A 32-year-old engineer enrolled at a nontraditional college in New York decided to use the computer science AP exam to earn low-level undergraduate credits in software. Even though three of the six credits were canceled out by similar credits already earned, the exam was still a credit-building bargain because of the small investment of money and preparation time. Passing with a grade of three, this engineer recalls the experience of taking the exam with a handful of high school students,

"Their AP instructor came into the room and patted their heads for luck. Before the exam started, I talked with the kids some and I realized we all wanted to pass and get those credits, but they were trying to get a head start on college, while I was trying to finish up."

Earn One-Fourth of a Degree from a GRE Subject Exam

Many people are familiar with the GRE general test, which is like an SAT test for college graduates that measures general knowledge in many areas. A GRE subject exam focuses on a single area of college level study (a major). As an example, a college senior about to graduate with a bachelor's degree in engineering would take the GRE engineering subject exam and have the scores mailed to the graduate schools at which he or she applied. Each school would consider the score as part of its admission process. For the purposes of earning credit, there are some nontraditional schools that will evaluate scores on a GRE subject exam for credit awards.

GRE subject exams are given in the following specific subject areas.

Biology	French	Physics
Chemistry	Geology	Political Science
Computer Science	History	Psychology
Economics	Literature	Sociology
Education	Mathematics	Spanish
Engineering	Music	

The tests are multiple-choice and are considered difficult but fair. They require about three hours to complete. The engineering, computer science, physics, and mathematics tests are the types that technical professionals are usually most prepared to take and which apply to their degree programs.

This GRE Computer Science exam is a good example of the content breakdown of a test.

- Software systems and methodology (35%)
- Computer organization and architecture (20%)
- Theory (20%)
- Computational mathematics (20%)

Programming examples in the test are written in the Pascal language, with a large emphasis on data structures, operating systems, computer architecture, and digital/Boolean logic.

The GRE subject score is a percentile, ranking all test participants in each subject area. As with other standardized exams, getting the best score isn't necessary to pass. At some schools, you only have to score in the upper two-thirds to earn 30 semester credits, 15 of them at the upper level. This means that about 65 percent of the test-takers could have higher scores and you would still earn the credits.

The total cost of the exam is approximately $40, which comes to $1.34 per credit hour. Compare this with the cost of attending any college full-time for one year, and you'll realize this is your best credit-building bargain.

Doing well on these exams is not difficult for those with knowledge equal to that taught in college classrooms and those who take the time to learn and prepare for the GRE subject exam on their own. A benefit of using GRE exams to earn credit is the significant amount of upper-level credits awarded (other standardized exams are usually evaluated as freshman/sophomore-level credits). Since GRE subject tests are relatively inexpensive, you may even consider taking a practice run just to get the feel of a test.

To build up general education/free elective-type course credits, nontraditional students should consider studying for a GRE subject exam outside their technical arenas. For example, the GRE history test is fairly specific, and study materials abound. At certain schools, passing this exam will earn a large number of nontechnical credits. Picking an interesting subject to study is important because the process of preparing for the exam will be less of a grind.

■ ■ ■

Example: How to Pass Four GRE Exams

People who have taken a GRE subject exam often wince and groan when asked to recall how it went. Another reaction is to tell a story about how difficult it was. If you choose to take a GRE exam, don't let outside opinions scare you. Consider this story of an East Coast student who completed his bachelor of science degree using GRE exams to earn a total of 120 semester credits (nearly an entire degree).

Spending an average of six months to prepare for each exam, he used the GRE practice exams to guide him in each subject area. When he encountered a question in the practice exam he couldn't answer, he researched the answer. Over the course of his study, his ability to answer significant numbers of questions grew steadily. When he felt prepared he took the exam, then after a short break, began study for the next one. After passing four different GRE subject exams, his graduation day was close at hand.

• • • • •

Most four-year colleges administer the GRE subject exams three or four times a year. Information is usually available from the testing office at nearby colleges or universities or directly from the Educational Testing Service.

The GRE is a credit-building method so attractive that it often influences the decision on what nontraditional college to attend. Even if you don't choose a school that accepts GRE exams directly for credit, a good GRE score might bolster a prior-learning portfolio.

13. In the state diagram below, the finite-state machine S has a starting state A and accepting state D. Which of the following regular expressions will be accepted by S?

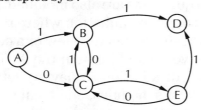

(A) 1(01)*(10)*1   (B) (10)*1   (C) (01)*1
    (D) (01)*(10)*   (E) 0(10)*

16. In this program fragment, with an arbitrary value for n

```
(1)  i = 1;
(2)  while i <= n do
        begin
(3)      a[i] := i;
(4)      i := i + 1;
        end
```

Let I represent the initialization in step (1), let T represent the test in line (2), let A represent the assignment in step 3, and let X represent the increment of i in step (4).

Of the following regular expressions, which one represents all possible normally terminated executions of the above code fragment?

(A) *(ITAX)**   (B) *I(TA)*X*   (C) *I(AXT)**
(D) *IAX(TAX)**   (E) None of the above

Questions in the Style of GRE Subject Examination
Computer Science

Graduate Record Subject Exam (GRE)
Educational Testing Service
P.O. Box 6004
Princeton, NJ 08541-6004
(609) 921-900

Course Credits from ACT PEP Exams

Another popular type of standardized tests was originally developed by Regents College in New York (they were administered in that state as Regents College Exams, or RCE) but are now given in all states as the American College Testing Proficiency Examination Program (ACT PEP). As with other exams, you may choose from a list of ACT PEP exams to determine if you can use one or more to earn credits applicable toward your degree program.

Before you register for ACT PEP exams, you can request and receive study guides for each test you are interested in taking. The study guide describes the exam length and scoring, content makeup (by percentage according to content area), a content outline, and reading recommendations. To give you a feel for the exam, sample exam questions are also included. ACT PEP is a way of earning credit through examination where the study areas are clearly defined for those who need review or a complete course of study. If interested, you should obtain the ACT PEP *Candidate Registration Guide*. In addition to having detailed registration information, forms, test schedules, and local testing sites, it contains an order form for the free study guides and other publications.

Exams are given at many colleges and universities four times a year. These exams are not as widely available as the CLEP exams, and test sites are further apart. Contact a local college testing office for further information.

The exams are multiple choice, short answer, and essay (or some combination thereof), and they require three to four hours to complete. Scores are mailed to the student and designated schools within six weeks for objective tests (no essay); if the test contained an essay or other written portion, exam results will arrive in eight to twelve weeks. Scores are scaled and expressed as a number; a score of 45 is often considered the cutoff point for passing. Credit earned for passing an ACT PEP exam ranges from three to fifteen semester credits, depending on the exam and the evaluating school. The cost varies, but most exams are administered for under $100.

Forty exams are available and are widely accepted as proof that credit should be awarded in various science, business, art, education, and nursing courses. Though there are no ACT PEP exams directly related to high technology, they often satisfy general education and elective requirements.

A note for strategic test-takers: One difference between ACT PEP and other exams is that there is no penalty for guessing (in most other exams, to discourage guessing, a percentage of a correct answer is deducted for every wrong answer). This is not to say the test is any easier to take or pass, but it's advantageous to answer every question even if it's a guess.

Carefully plan and use your time before taking ACT PEP exams. Since many of these tests cover more than the material covered in one college course, they require more preparation than typical standardized exams. Since the test locations are spread out, be

OBLIGING ACT PEP

ACT PEP is long on convenience for all test-takers. Here are a few other ACT PEP offers you'll want to consider.

First is an excellent free publication, *Preparing to Do Your Best on the ACT PEP Examinations*. Besides discussing ACT PEP examinations, it contains many tips valuable to anyone using standardized tests, including study plans along with suggestions for attitude, mental, and physical preparation. It is available by contacting ACT.

Each exam's study guide recommends textbooks to study for ACT PEP tests. A large selection of these texts can be ordered by phone 24 hours a day, seven days a week. This service is provided by the Empire State College External Program Bookstore, which accepts MasterCard and Visa.

prepared to travel farther to take these exams. And since the scores for some exams may be three months in coming, don't schedule an ACT PEP exam close to an expected graduation date.

ACT PEP Exams
American College Testing Program
P.O. Box 4014
2255 North Dubuque Road
Iowa City, IA 52243
(319) 337-1363

SUNY Empire State College External Programs Bookstore
5 Grande Boulevard
Saratoga Springs, NY 12866-9060
(800) 338-9719

Use DANTES Exams to Avoid Classes

Although active military personnel and veterans have always been able to take exams from DANTES, since 1983 civilians too have been using these exams to earn credit. DANTES (also referred to as DANTES Standardized Subject Tests or DSST) also offers a few exams in technical disciplines.

Armed forces personnel can arrange to have tests administered at military sites by contacting the nearest Base Education Center. Civilians need to make arrangements directly with a local college testing office to take the exam. Not all colleges administer the test, so it might take a few calls to locate a testing site where you can register; if all else fails, contact DANTES at the Educational Testing Service (ETS) and ask for the DANTES Registration Bulletin. There is no set schedule for DANTES exams. This flexibility is valuable since you can make arrangements to take exams when you're truly prepared.

When you take DANTES multiple-choice exams, there is no time limit. The idea is that you should finish the whole exam. Ninety minutes is usually enough time, but additional time is given as needed. It takes about three weeks for you and your degree-granting school to receive scores. Scores are scaled; minimum cutoff for credit varies with each exam and each school, but passing scores are approximately 50. The cost of each exam varies depending on your status (military or civilian); for civilians, it's typically less than $50.

Most of the exams earn from three to six semester credits, many at the upper (junior/senior) level. The DANTES exams have been evaluated by the American Council on Education, which publishes

PLAN AHEAD WHEN USING DANTES

When you register for DANTES testing through a college testing office, the college usually orders the materials from ETS and receives them about two weeks later. The exam materials, completed or not, must be sent back to ETS within 30 days. Within that time frame, you must arrange to take the test.

recommended credit awards. These are recommendations that each college can choose to use or adjust according to the needs of its degree programs. Credit awards for these exams are widely available at nontraditional schools.

There are approximately 50 DANTES exams in the following categories: mathematics, physical science, applied technology, business, social science, humanities, and foreign languages.

Of particular value to technical degree programs are Fundamentals of Electronics, Electric Circuits, Electronic Devices, Principles of Electronic Communications, Technical Writing, programming, and appropriate math and physics exams. If you have vocational training, quite a few of these exams may present a way for you to turn knowledge into college credit. If you are knowledgeable in recent history and culture, consider some recently added general education exams on subjects such as the Vietnam war, the environment, politics, and health.

■■■

Example: Everyone Can Use DANTES

Don't shy away from DANTES exams because they were originally designed for the military. This exam program is open to all interested in earning credit. A student in New Jersey, completing a nontraditional BS degree in information systems, earned 33 credits using standardized exams, including many offered by DANTES.

•••••

DANTES Examination Program
Educational Testing Service
Princeton, NJ 08541
(800) 257-9484

Other Exams to Get Your Degree Sooner

Different nontraditional colleges will accept different ranges of standardized exams for credit. Some schools will accept exams that are relatively obscure compared to the previously described methods. While these exams may not be widely available, it is worthwhile to understand all the standardized tests your school will consider for credit awards.

One example of a lesser-known exam is the New York University Proficiency Testing in Foreign Language. Certain colleges will accept a satisfactory score on this exam as proof that you know a foreign language and will award up to 12 semester credits. Over 25

EARLY DANTES EXAMS

Though they are now administered by ETS, prior to 1974 DANTES exams were administered by the U.S. Armed Forces Institute (USAFI). If you believe you passed exams before 1974, transcripts (as well as other information) can still be obtained from ETS.

In 1979, scoring systems for some tests were changed; don't panic if you have exam scores from that era that are much lower than today's passing scores. Alert your advisor if your exams had a prefix of SA or SB, and the scores will be adjusted to current equivalents.

languages are tested, with each exam covering three foreign language skills: verbal, written, and translation (into English). This exam can be taken almost anywhere—wherever you can arrange to have the exam proctored: colleges, service bases, foreign embassies, etc.

A second example is the TOCT exam, where people with demonstrated knowledge equal to that of vocational teachers can earn up to 60 semester credits at certain colleges.

New York University
School of Continuing Education
Proficiency Testing in Foreign Languages
Foreign Languages Department
2 University Place, Room 55
Washington Square
New York, NY 10003
(212) 998-1212

TOCT
409 Bishop Hall
Ferris State University
Big Rapids, MI 49307
(616) 796-4695

College Credits from Training You've Already Received

Turn Company-Sponsored Training into College Credits

Your completion of training courses at work (or other seminars from noncollegiate institutions) may be worth credit. It's a pleasant surprise to find out training paid for by a past or present employer can earn college credit—in some cases, significant amounts of it. Thousands of students have earned tens of thousands of credits using this method.

You can start this process by gathering all your training completion certificates. If you haven't been saving these certificates, get them by contacting the personnel or human resources departments at past and present employers (you can help by supplying a list of training you've completed). Inspect all the certificates and make sure each specifies the training class title, date given, and it's location. Next you need to determine if the courses were evaluated by a PONSI organization for college-level credit. Ways to find this out include:

- Asking the sponsoring organization
- Asking your company to find out
- Looking in a PONSI guide
- Contacting PONSI organizations
- Asking your college advisor for help

When the PONSI-evaluated courses have been identified, concentrate on getting credit for them by having the sponsoring organizations send official training transcripts to the college where you've matriculated. The transcripts will enable your advisor to review and award credit as appropriate. When credit is put on your transcript, it is awarded in certain subject areas and is usually put in as a pass, not computed in your grade point average. Costs for this evaluation are minimal; they're either included as part of the annual enrollment fee or charged at the same rate as for transferring college courses.

QUICK GUIDE TO COMPANY-SPONSORED TRAINING

Training sponsored by industry and other training organizations can be evaluated for college-level credit. The process of getting credit is simple: Submit proof to your transcript evaluator that you've successfully completed training evaluated by a Programs on Noncollegiate Sponsored Instruction (PONSI) organization. If you determine that training you've had has been evaluated by a PONSI organization, then sending documentation to your transcript evaluator begins the process that can put credits on your transcript. The cost of having these credits put on your transcript is minimal (about the same as transfer credit) for directly evaluated training.

Reasons to use: capitalizes on previous training, low cost, evaluation is formalized

Possible restrictions: certificate of completion must be found for training

Look for: applicability to degree program

To better understand how this credit-building method works, it's helpful to see how one of the PONSI organizations operates. Since 1974, the American Council on Education (ACE) PONSI has conducted evaluations of civilian training programs in much the same way it's committed to reviewing military training. If appropriate, training is equated to a recommended amount of college credits and is published in the *National Guide to Educational Credit for Training Programs*. This ACE PONSI guide contains recommendations for thousands of training courses that are sponsored by more than 100 businesses and training organizations.

It isn't necessary to own the *National Guide* because it's widely used by traditional and nontraditional schools that accept training for credit. (If you need to review it, check at your public library or ask a local college if you can use their copy). The recommended amount of credit listed in the *National Guide* leaves the final credit award (which can go up or down) to the discretion of each school. In a case where a student does exceptionally well in the training program, the award could be higher than recommended in the *National Guide*. Despite the latitude given to credit-granting institutions, this is generally a very formalized process.

The other PONSI organization is the National Program on Noncollegiate Sponsored Instruction (National PONSI), which is associated with the University of the State of New York and publishes its own directory, *College Credit Recommendations*. ACE PONSI and National PONSI have evaluated different training programs with little overlap, but determining if your training was evaluated for credit is not as easy as looking in both of these books. You'll need more background to understand how evaluated training can disappear from these directories but still be worth credit.

PONSI TRANSCRIPT SERVICES

Another way to prove credits is to use registry services associated with the main PONSI organizations. If the group that sponsored your training belongs to a registry, it will have a record of your training completion. In this case, all you have to do is have the registry send a transcript to your school for credit evaluation.

ACE PONSI and National PONSI evaluate training programs and regularly review evaluations for a fee, which is mentioned not to imply any crassness to the process, but to explain that PONSI credit recommendations can "disappear" when the training institution declines to continue its active membership in the evaluating PONSI. For example, say you've completed a course in telecommunications sponsored by your company back in 1989 that at the time was evaluated for credit and listed in one of the two directories. If your company decided in 1991 to not have the evaluation updated (for any number of reasons—perhaps because of the associated expense), then the subsequent directory would not list the course for recommended credit. However, the earlier evaluations can still be used by your school to determine a credit award. The trick is to check all the directories.

As stated before, evaluated courses are reviewed to make sure they are still worthy of PONSI recommendation. Courses may be decertified if they change or are deemed unworthy. This is why the date of course completion is as important as the course name when the evaluator attempts to make a credit award.

Many of the evaluated training programs are in the high-tech arena: nuclear engineering, telecommunications, programming, computer programming operations, and hundreds of other areas. However, a technical student should not disregard other types of training received. Every credit usually helps, so it pays to round up all training completion certificates.

Suppose you find that your training was evaluated for credit by a PONSI organization not directly recognized by your school. One way around this is to see if the PONSI organization can convert its credit recommendations into a college transcript, which can be done when it is affiliated with a college. By getting credit on an official college transcript, you improve the likelihood that you can get credit onto your transcript using the normal transfer process.

Companies that supply their employees with training can often be convinced to choose the type of training that results in college credit. You shouldn't count on this as part of a degree plan, but it doesn't hurt to ask your employer.

Behind PONSI-recommended credit is one of the biggest changes in postsecondary education: Degree-granting institutions now recognize that corporations are doing a good job of providing college-level education. Earlier there were some problems getting PONSI credit accepted, but today it is commonly used.

For any training that is not evaluated by PONSI, you should still hang onto your certificates; you may be able to use them as part of the prior learning credit-building method.

■ ■ ■

Example: Using Training for Credit

The following is a typical surprise success story. A network supervisor employed by AT&T had taken numerous training courses sponsored by her company. After she enrolled in a nontraditional school, the initial transcript evaluation converted that training into 12 semester credits. She challenged the original review and wound up with a total of 15 credits from corporate training—the equivalent of five courses or one semester of full-time coursework.

• • • • •

 FUTURE TRAINING CREDITS AT WORK

Have you ever wondered if the training developed by your company is extensive enough to be worth college credit? It may be helpful to have your training officer consider contracting with one of the PONSI organizations for an evaluation. Evaluation can be a slow process, so it isn't recommended as a credit-building strategy, but if you help get the process started, you can leave a legacy for those coming after you.

PONSI Organizations

American Council on Education (ACE)
Program on Noncollegiate Sponsored Instruction
One Dupont Circle
Washington, DC 20036

The National Program on Noncollegiate Sponsored Instruction
Cultural Education Center, Room 5A25
Empire State Plaza
Albany, NY 12230
(518) 434-0118

PONSI Registries

Regents College PONSI Transcript Service
1450 Western Avenue
Albany, NY 12203-3524
(518) 474-3703

ACE Registry of Credit Recommendations
One Dupont Circle
Washington, DC 20036
(202) 833-4920

QUICK GUIDE TO CERTIFICATES AND LICENSES

Certain professional licenses or certificates are accepted by many nontraditional schools as the equivalent of college-level credit. If you have such credentials (or intend to get them), have official documentation sent to your transcript evaluator. Costs for having these credits put on your transcript are about the same as for transfer credit.

Reasons to use: low cost, some schools evaluate directly, can generate years' worth of credit

Possible restrictions: not all schools evaluate directly

Look for: alternate methods such as using certificates in portfolio assessment

---

Earn Credit from Professional Certificates and Licenses

A professional certificate establishes that an individual is qualified to practice in a certain profession. Many professionals (particularly in the medical, business, and information system fields) are required by law to obtain certificates. At certain schools, these certificates are directly evaluated for credit. The same holds true for licenses, including Federal Aviation Administration (FAA) licenses.

If you have (or believe you could obtain) a professional license or certificate, you should find schools that accept this credit-building method. You should also become familiar with what each license you intend to use is worth (in credits and in what subject area). When enrolled in a school that directly evaluates certificates and licenses, you begin the evaluation process by sending the transcript evaluator copies of the certificate. As with college transcripts, you also arrange to have the training sponsor send in official documentation (results of exams and coursework) related to the certificate or license award.

Recommendations for credit awards are up to the individual schools, but ACE provides some guidelines. When the evaluator completes the evaluation of your certificate or license, you are sent a credit award notice and the credit is placed on your transcript. Credit awarded depends on the license or certificate. The credit is entered on your transcript as a passing grade; it won't be figured into the grade point average. Cost is usually equivalent to what the degree-granting institution charges for incoming transfer credit.

Certificates that have been evaluated for credit include those used by computer professionals (Certified Data Processor, Certificate of Computer Programming, and Certified Systems Professional) and power plant operators (reactor operator licenses). Medical professionals such as radiation technicians, EMTs, and respiratory therapists can earn, in some cases, more than a year's worth of credit. FAA licenses ranging from Private Pilot to Air Traffic Controller also count. While some of these areas may not seem to apply to technical degrees, remember that degree programs have plenty of free electives. People wanting to switch careers (from secretary to software engineer, for example) might find that a professional certificate can get them a credit-building head start and become motivated to actually begin.

A student who matriculates in a school that doesn't directly award credit for certificates and licenses is encouraged to consider a portfolio assessment (prior learning) strategy, using their certificate license as evidence.

One technique that has been used is to study and pass certificate exams in a deliberate effort to earn credit. For example, if you attain a Certified Data Processor certificate, it alone could be worth up to 36 semester credits at some schools. This would be well worth your study effort because you end up with a certificate that is valuable to your career.

■ ■ ■

Example: License to Graduate

An energetic and under-challenged high school student simultaneously attended a local junior college. At the same time he graduated from high school, he received an associate's degree. After starting work, his manager told him about an external degree program in computer software offered by a nontraditional school. He enrolled and quickly used the Institute for Certification of Computer Professionals (ICCP) license exam to get an Associate Computer Professional license and a GRE exam to earn another full year of college credit. While working full-time providing contract computer support for the Coast Guard, he was able to earn his BS degree before he turned 21.

• • • • •

LICENSES AND CERTIFICATES USED FOR CREDIT AWARDS

Business Certificates

Associate Computer Professional (ACP) (ICCP)

Certificate in Computer Programming (ICCP)

Certified Data Processor (CDP) (ICCP)

Certified Employee Benefit Specialist (CEBS)

Certified Financial Planner (CFP)

Certified Professional Secretary (CPS)

Certified Public Accountant (CPA)

Certified Public Manager Program of New Jersey (CPM)

Certified Purchasing Manager (CPM)

Certified Systems Professional (CSP) (ICCP)

Chartered Financial Consultant (ChFC)

Chartered Life Underwriter (CLU)

Chartered Property Casualty Underwriter (CPCU)

Aviation Licenses and Certificates

FAA Airplane Transport Pilot

FAA Air Traffic Control Specialist

FAA Flight Engineer, Dispatcher or Navigator

FAA Instructor, Airplane or Instrument Rating

FAA Mechanic Rating for Airframe and/or Power Plant

FAA Multiengine Airplane

continued on next page

Credit Awards from Military Training and Service Ratings

One of the largest providers of training in the U.S. is the armed forces. Training is given in course form, or as comprehensive preparation for a military occupation. Getting credit for military experience is routine and accepted at most nontraditional institutions. In the following descriptions, the term *training* is used to describe both military courses and service occupations.

As with transfer credit (from accredited schools), in military training, the student supplies a transcript evaluator with information. The evaluator verifies that training was received and then determines a credit award using guidelines from ACE. Since transcripts may come from the government, students should prepare to do more paperwork and spend more time getting transcripts to their transcript evaluators.

Proof of training completion can be supplied to transcript evaluators in a number of ways.

- *Navy Ratings*: Active-duty personnel should send the transcript evaluator a certified copy of DD Form 295 (obtained from the Base Education Office). Veterans with Navy Ratings should send discharge report DD 214; if this cannot be found, they should contact the GSA/National Personnel Records Center.

- *Army training*: Active-duty personnel should send the transcript evaluator a certified copy of DD Form 295 (from the Base Education Office). Veterans with Army training should send discharge report DD 214; if this cannot be found, they should contact the GSA/National Personnel Records Center. ACE and the Army have a training registry for active personnel and veterans who began service after October 1981. Students can get this transcript at no charge by using DA Form 5454-R (available from the school where matriculated) or by directing a request to the Army/ACE Registry Transcript Service office.

- *Army Military Occupational Specialty* (MOS): Active-duty personnel should send the transcript evaluator a certified copy of USAEEC Form 10A or EER (obtained from the Base Education Office). Veterans with Army MOS should contact the GSA/National Personnel Records Center for a copy of USAEEC Form 10A.

- *Army Warrant Office MOS*: Active-duty personnel and veterans should send the transcript evaluators certified copies of either DA Form 2-1 or DA Form 66. Active-duty personnel can obtain these forms from the Base Education Office; veterans should contact the GSA/National Personnel Records Center.

- *Air Force training*: Personnel who served before 1972 should submit form DD 214 to the transcript evaluator; personnel who served during or after 1972 should arrange to have a transcript sent from the Community College of the Air Force.

- *Marine Corps MOS*: Personnel should send the transcript evaluator the Individual Duty Area Qualification Summary Sheet.

Documentation needs can vary depending on your school, so check with your advisor to understand all the requirements. In addition to the paper documentation, the evaluating school may require you to take a test or interview to establish that the training received meets the school's own standards. A good approach if you are discharged or retired from the service is to have all military training evaluated first, then see how it fits into the degree program. Military credit is often entered on the transcript as a pass, so it's not used to compute the overall grade point average. The cost for military credit is usually evaluated at the same rate as college transfer credit. Active-duty personnel and veterans may be eligible for significant fee reductions, in-state status, and other financial aid.

ACE established credit recommendations in its *Guide to the Evaluation of Educational Experiences in the Armed Services*. This four-volume set has become the standard reference for college evaluators of military training. ACE has done this since 1945, so even students who were discharged long ago may earn credit. Course-by-course, occupation-by-occupation credit is recommended for the various service branches: Army, Air Force, Navy, Marine Corps, Coast Guard, and the Department of Defense. The increasing use of technology in the military means that many can get a big credit-building boost from service training.

■■■

Example: Using Military Training

Navy Nuclear Power School provides a large part of the training sailors receive to prepare them to crew a nuclear submarine. If you have this training, what type of course credits could you expect to have already earned? The following table shows, in general, what military training can mean to your transcript.

continued from previous page

FAA Private, Commercial or Instrument Pilot Airplane

FAA Private, Commercial or Instrument Rotocraft Pilot

Medical and Therapy Licenses

Histotechnology

New Jersey EMT Ambulance, New Jersey EMT Paramedic

Nuclear Medicine Technology

Radiation Therapy Technology

Radiologic Technology

Registered Nurse

Respiratory Therapist

Respiratory Therapy Technician

Miscellaneous Licenses and Certificates

Evelyn Wood Reading Dynamics

Surveyor License

Nuclear Certificates and Licenses

National Registry of Radiation Protection Technologists

Navy Nuclear Power School (see Military Credit)

NRC Reactor Operator

NRC Senior Reactor Operator

Approximate Credit Earned by Military Training

Course	Credits
Mathematics	4
Physics I, II	6
Chemistry	3
Atomic physics	3
Nuclear physics	3
Nuclear materials	2
Heat transfer, fluids	3
Thermodynamics	2
Radiological fundamentals	2
Reactor technology	3

This totals more than a year of full-time work. Of course, not all military training is worth this much credit, but many people with past military training have discovered that their experience was worth a surprising number of credits at accredited schools.

Credit can also be earned for these specialized operator training ratings: Machinist Mate, Electronics Technician, Electrician Mate, and Interior Communications.

.....

QUICK GUIDE TO MILITARY CREDIT

Military training and occupation ratings have been evaluated for credit by ACE. These evaluations are used as guidelines to determine credit awards. Military transcripts and discharge papers are examples of documentation needed for verification of training. Cost is equivalent to transfer credit. Credit awarded depends on the military training.

Reasons to use: low cost, easy evaluation and transfer

Possible restrictions: military paperwork and records required from the government, nonapplicability to degree program

Look for: accomplished military training evaluators

For courses and service occupations not in the *Guide*, students may consider using prior learning evaluation to earn credit. Everything else in this chapter applies to active personnel, veterans, students who served reserve stints, and even civilians who took military training courses (i.e., spouses of those in the service taking military training). Again, credit awards for military training are well known to academic advisors. Assistance in preparing forms and ordering transcripts can be readily obtained from the school where the student is matriculated.

■ ■ ■

Example: Pulling Rank

One student in the military earned 75 percent of the credits toward his bachelor's degree using nontraditional methods. Because of his enlisted classification as an Electronics Chief Petty Officer, the credit award recommended in the ACE *Guide* didn't apply to the core area of study. As a result, this student applied the credits in the liberal arts electives component.

.....

For a DD214 discharge report, contact:

General Services Administration (GSA)
National Personnel Records Center
Military Personnel Records
9700 Page Boulevard
St. Louis, MO 63132

Army/ACE Registry Transcript Service (AARTS)
Ft. Leavenworth, KS 66027-5073

Community College of the Air Force
Building 836
Maxwell Air Force Base, AL 36112-6655

Turn What You Know into College Credits

Prior Learning and Portfolio Assessment

The following statement is easily refuted: The only way people gain college-level ability is from college courses. Actually, if one could wave a magic wand that awarded college credit for knowledge gained as part of living (working, reading, hobbies, travel, volunteering, and other experiences), millions of people would find themselves with newly found officially sanctioned credit hours. This would be especially true for technically up-to-date professionals. If you thought the only way to earn credit for experienced-based learning was to give in and take conventional courses, don't despair. While you can't use a magic wand, there is a method: Prior learning can be evaluated for credit. More than 1,000 schools in the U.S. evaluate experience-based learning for credit. This is a technique that has grown in popularity, reaching more traditional schools every year.

Evaluation of prior learning can be complex; those interested in using this method should look not only for schools that evaluate, but also for those that provide students with sufficient training and administrative support. When in doubt about a school, ask to speak with students who have used, or are using, this method.

It takes a fair amount of effort and preparation to translate your experience into technical and general education credits, but this credit-building method has been formalized and used at nontraditional schools for decades. In fact, this is one of the most traditional of nontraditional credit-building methods. There are two primary methods of evaluation: portfolio assessment and examination assessment. Before these evaluation methods are explained further, it's wise to examine the main types of evaluation models used by individual schools.

The most straightforward and popular evaluation model is where knowledge is evaluated against established college course content

QUICK GUIDE TO PRIOR LEARNING CREDIT

Credit can be earned for learning that occurs outside a formal environment: employment, hobbies, travel, reading, and volunteer work. Documentation is provided by the student to prove college-level and associate learning to college-level courses. Credit awards are based on evaluation of documentation (or other presentation), and the cost often is inexpensive per credit hour.

Reasons to use: low cost, establishes creditworthiness of real-world learning

Possible restrictions: time and effort to prepare, process is subjective

Look for: sponsored courses that direct preparation of portfolios, competent administrative support as described in college course catalogs. For example, a mechanical engineer with extensive knowledge using finite element analysis would have his experience evaluated against a college course in the same subject. A variation on this model is where the student's knowledge is evaluated against a degree curriculum (or a major part of a degree). Schools using this model typically require the student to identify and provide equivalent college course descriptions as part of the evaluation.

Another evaluation model exists that is not so tied to typical college courses and degree programs. Imagine an engineer who has completed in-depth study, application, and teaching of practical, yet challenging, Total Quality Management (TQM) techniques. Few college courses are taught in this area; in fact, not many engineering degree programs address real-life process improvement issues or methods. Still, if the complexity of TQM material equals the complexity of college-level learning and is relevant to a particular degree, certain institutions will evaluate that type of experience in their prior learning programs. You can tell that a school uses this method by the more elaborate preparation and creativity required in the evaluation process.

Portfolio assessment is a popular method of prior learning evaluation. The student prepares a portfolio designed to inventory, describe, and prove prior learning knowledge. The finished portfolio is submitted to the college for assessment. The assessment might award all, part, or none of the credit the student attempted to document in the portfolio.

Portfolio assessment is usually a well-structured process. Schools prefer to see portfolios in a consistent format, so it's typical to require the student to undergo an orientation and training course prior to portfolio development.

What are some of the elements in a portfolio? If a school evaluates knowledge against college courses, the portfolio should contain copies of course descriptions from college catalogs of any accredited institutions. These descriptions will establish course content and typical credit awards. Evidence of your knowledge is a key part of the portfolio; professional licenses, news clippings, patents, performance reviews, letters of recommendation, design documents, and invention disclosures are just a few examples of proof. Also included in a portfolio is an essay (or set of essays) describing knowledge gained, the story behind the learning, and related evidence. One technical portfolio I've seen was three inches thick, but the bulk of it was copies of the supplied notes from more than a dozen training courses. This portfolio was shown to me because it was considered exemplary, but each student is not expected to generate an entire document of that size.

Examination assessment may include the development of a portfolio to describe knowledge gained, but the end result is that the student must take an exam or series of exams to establish that knowledge actually exists. The school develops the exams especially for each student. They can be written, oral, or both. Success or failure on the exam determines the credit award.

■ ■ ■

Example: Experience vs. Learning

Prior learning evaluation criteria includes the following factor: How much does the student understand underlying academic principles to back up practical, hands-on experience? The mix of theory and practice varies depending on the area of learning, but an example will help explain the basic concept. Many software engineers are skilled enough to create simple digital hardware systems from specs supplied by semiconductor manufacturers—for example, hooking up integrated circuits (IC) in a design suggested by the IC vendor. However, designs of this sort don't necessarily constitute learning equivalent to what is taught in a digital logic course. The principles of digital design require an understanding of semiconductor theory, Boolean algebra, and many other areas. Using prior learning, a software engineer hoping to get credit for a digital logic course could improve his or her chances by being able to present original circuit designs and further proof of knowledge in the essential academic topics.

• • • • •

The guidelines of ACE about extrainstitutional (experience-based) learning specifically state that experience is not enough to earn credit. The emphasis at the college must be on evaluation of the learning, and determining if this learning is college-level and relevant to the student's course of study. The implications: First, a student has to know the material, and second, the student will be judged against a college curriculum.

Whenever credit is awarded, the school notifies the student and places credit on the transcript. It's perfectly legitimate to use a college for only its prior learning evaluation service and then transfer that same credit to another school. Cost is usually computed based on the amount of credit awarded. Since the cost is associated mainly with the evaluation, the equivalent cost per credit hour can be a fraction of that for classroom courses. When blocks of credit are awarded, prior learning can also be a time-saver when compared with many other methods, especially traditional study.

There are many elements to successful portfolio assessment, but with training and diligence in execution, most students find it an effective credit-building method. Some schools are claiming a 90 percent success rate—that is, 90 percent of the students are granted credits as a result of portfolio assessment.

The less confident you are of preparing a portfolio on your own, the more you should seek out a college that requires a portfolio development course. The main benefit is that the course will allow you to translate your life experiences into a presentation acceptable to the college. Another benefit is that you can be given credit for completing the portfolio course itself.

When looking for a school to evaluate prior learning, remember that more schools are offering this method of earning credit, but many schools do not offer a comprehensive evaluation program. There's quite a difference between schools offering comprehensive evaluation programs in many academic areas and other institutions that have limited evaluation programs. The difference is measured in the amount of learning you may be able to get evaluated for credit. Technical professionals shouldn't underestimate the many areas of learning outside their specialized realm that have been evaluated for credit. Public speaking, management, and technical writing are areas in which many people have developed skills.

Look for restrictions concerning portfolio assessment even at schools that permit the use of this method. One example is when a school won't allow the use of prior learning for course prerequisites when the course itself has already been completed. If you're aware of this situation, you could get the prior learning credit first and then take the course.

There are no guarantees with prior learning methods. Significant amounts of credit can be earned, but the evaluation process may be too subjective for some students. Some students may be frustrated by the fact that years of employment can translate to zero college credits; it's college-level learning, not mere seniority, that counts.

To illustrate, compare an electronics technician who merely does his job for 15 years to another technician, with only five years of experience, who accomplishes much in software projects outside her hardware job description through the steady acquisition of theory and application of new computer and programming skills. The technician with five years experience is in a much better position to claim the acquisition of college-level learning.

✓
PUBLICATIONS

The Council for Adult and Experiential Learning (CAEL) is a nonprofit organization that works to promote and expand lifelong learning opportunities for adults and to advance experiential learning and its assessment. It publishes a variety of books to help adults learn how to have their prior learning assessed. If you are seriously considering earning credit for your prior learning, contact CAEL for a list of publications and a current price list.

Inexpensively turning learning into credit is reason enough to use this method for large blocks of learning. It can also be a good catch-all technique where others have failed or come up short. For example, some transfer credit may be denied because of course age. However, if the student can use portfolio credit to establish that knowledge is current, having to retake the course is avoided.

Council for Adult and Experiential Learning (CAEL)
223 West Jackson, Suite 510
Chicago, IL 60606
(312) 922-5909

Create Your Own College Courses and Custom Degree Programs

Individualized Degree Programs

Here is where a nontraditional student with specific goals and a healthy appetite for learning can have fun while earning a college degree. Designing your own college curriculum isn't the fastest way to earn credit or a degree, but this learning style can provide a more satisfying educational process. Imagine studying a rapidly evolving technology, applying it on the job, and ending up with increased status at work and a degree.

This open or individualized learning is not just a credit-building method, it's also a degree program. Because of this, a mandatory first step is finding and gaining acceptance at a college or university that offers this option. This is the most unstructured credit-building method, and procedures vary widely between schools. Because of this, it's wise to research individualized degree programs in-depth at more than one institution. Attempt to find a school with a faculty that can adequately sponsor and support you in your field of study. An advisor with a sociology background is not going to be of much help in the study of computer architecture. Some of the programs that exist use the term *university without walls* to, in part, tell you that something about this offering differs from the norm.

Assuming you find a school and are accepted for enrollment, the process of putting together your degree program and completion plan remains. Planning your own courses (or individualized study) usually requires face-to-face meetings, so a 100 percent external open degree is rare. To accommodate distant students, some colleges arrange special weekend or one-week sessions for planning and meeting with faculty. Putting together a learning plan is often so extensive that it's considered part of the learning process; it can take up to a quarter or semester of effort. Learning plans can be quite lengthy, some as long as dozens of pages. (Compare this to the two pages in a college catalog that explain most degree programs). The learning plan is reviewed, and, when approved, becomes the basis by which the degree is completed.

The learning plan can include many methods of earning credit, including all of the ones discussed in the previous chapters, but the use of independent projects, internships, seminars, and work-based learning makes these programs unique. The concentration in the learning plan can focus on multiple areas of studies or explore one subject in a broader academic context. For example, in software development, an applications-user interface is effective not just because the programming is technically sound, but because common aspects of human nature and cognition are understood. As such, an individualized degree program entitled Ergonomic Object-Oriented User Interfaces might be designed by the student to study object-oriented software, psychology, and physiology.

For those willing to do the work, the individualized study method is a way to make the liberal arts component of a degree program more integrated or relevant to the technical course of study. The angle is to identify some soft aspect of what it is you intend to study and then propose to study its aspects. An example of the cross-discipline approach to degree program design: Instead of completing study in electrical engineering, you would work in a component that studies organizational aspects of technology-development groups. Information processing is not an isolated topic when you consider the effects of productivity and social adjustment of moving from mainframes to distributed processing and client/server environments.

How do schools evaluate studies if they are planned by the student? Though it sounds like the fox guarding the henhouse, there are usually plenty of reviews of work progress, plus the same type of portfolio preparation for prior learning credit is generally required. In fact, schools can offer the option of portfolio study as an extension of portfolio assessment. Again, this evaluation process can increase the time it takes to earn credits.

To complete learning in open degree programs, the student is not required to complete all work as part of self-directed study. Many of the other methods are usually used in conjunction with individualized study.

Creating your own college course is potentially the most rewarding educational experience because you can design it to fit your interests, with the reward of larger blocks of credit. This free-spirited cousin of independent study has a price: You have to design the course as well as complete it, which takes time and additional administrative work with the college faculty and staff.

THE LEFT STUFF

What is a school looking for when it evaluates students for matriculation in an individualized degree? These programs are meant for entrepreneurs of learning. Work is planned and evaluated by a faculty sponsor, but the intent is that the student has specific education goals that can't be met by traditional programs. Quite often, a student who's a huge success in individualized study degree programs may have been stifled to the point of failure in standard degree programs.

Typically, there is back-and-forth communication when designing the course, scoping educational goals, and agreeing on a method of feedback (to gauge progress and evaluate). Expect some additional costs; these programs can be very expensive.

Many graduate degree programs use this method because the potential students find the timing right. After completing their bachelor's degrees, many students feel ready to pursue areas of their own interest. This is especially true of technical professionals who have been in the workforce for a long time and have an idea for a master's-level study area that fits into their career plans.

In the world of technical employment, there are many opportunities to design a learning program, so many technology students look no further than their own work area for inspiration. If, for example, a student's company is considering automating a portion of a factory process, an impressive list of credit-worthy learning experiences can be derived (and perhaps directed) by the student: robotics, computer networks, statistics, queuing theory, test engineering, programming, and system integration.

Look for New and Obscure Ways to Earn Credit

New methods of earning credit are introduced every few years. Other less popular methods have been around for years. When choosing a college, review its materials carefully and look for new or unusual credit-building methods beyond those described here.

An example of an additional credit-building method: Some colleges and universities grant credit for a college course if the student has taught a similar course at an accredited college-level institution.

In the future, don't be surprised to see technology used more often to help evaluate college-level learning. For example, in a variety of subjects, it will soon be possible to take a computer-based test, where the computer can dynamically adjust the questions asked based on previous question responses (more difficult questions if there are many correct answers, easier questions if there are many incorrect answers). This type of test could accurately gauge student knowledge in minutes instead of hours.

The greatest new opportunities in nontraditional credit-building will probably occur in the area of graduate study. In the previously mentioned credit-building descriptions, it's obvious that many methods are aimed primarily at the undergraduate level. This will change as the population matures and industry increases its demand for employees with postbaccalaureate degrees.

STATISTICS FROM INDIVIDUALIZED PROGRAMS

A university with an individualized program has produced some interesting statistics concerning its BA and BS students.

- Approximately 60 percent are accepted at good graduate schools.
- An amazing 75 percent end up directly employed in the area of their education. (This number is usually much lower in normal degree programs.) This is probably an indication that the passion that inspired students' individualized study carried over into employment in the same area.
- More than 94 percent are admitted to the graduate school of their first choice.

11

Focus on Key Methods to Improve Credit-Earning Efforts

After discovering the range of alternative credit-building methods described in the previous chapters, most people find they are interested in only a few methods, perhaps even a single method. A person with much experience and accumulated knowledge may read about prior learning/portfolio assessment and rejoice at the realization that he or she can earn credit for experiential learning. Others may have less knowledge, but sense that they would be able to direct their own study, so they choose independent study and standardized exams. At this point, you need to critically evaluate credit-building methods against your own objectives and circumstances. The plan is to identify the primary credit-building methods that you can most successfully use toward your degree completion.

Should You Choose Your School First?

It may seem premature to choose your credit-building methods first; it may appear more reasonable to first settle on a school with which to matriculate. However, nontraditional institutions vary in which credit-earning methods they accept. You might choose a college or university based on reputation, cost, or other factors, only to find that the school doesn't permit the use of a credit-building method you desired. Almost by definition, the nontraditional student is most interested in finding a school that accepts credit-building methods most likely to lead to graduation.

If this objective of selecting the credit-building method makes sense in this context but still seems a bit unusual, it might be because this approach is different than the traditional method, where a student chooses a school based on reputation. For the traditional student this method is fine, since most traditional schools are uniform in their academic programs: The only credit-building method is the classroom.

Most nontraditional students end up using a mixture of methods to complete degree requirements, but if the student needs to obtain one or more years of college credits, then the bulk of credits are usually earned by one to three key methods. The reason for this is that students gravitate to primary methods most suitable and efficient for them.

Following thorough study of the various credit-earning methods, you should start to evaluate local colleges and universities. Many of the nontraditional credit-earning methods will be available at institutions in your area; in addition to discovering these local options, you'll be able to explore some of the methods as actually practiced by schools. Also, remember that some methods, such as independent study, will require the use of local proctors and other resources, so identifying and establishing contact with schools in your area can be as important to degree completion as selecting a primary credit-building method.

Estimate How Much Credit You Already Have

Establishing how much credit you already have can help you determine the major areas of credit earning you'll need to focus on. A common mistake concerning previous college-level credits is in trying to remember what coursework has been completed. The tendency is to underestimate how much has been completed. The best practice is to write the registrar's office at each school you've attended and ask for a copy of a complete transcript of credit. Keep in mind that colleges and universities are operating under guidelines that prohibit them from sending your transcripts without proper authorization. You, of course, have the authority to see your own transcript, but the request usually must be written, bear your signature, and include identifying information. Many schools charge a transcript fee from $1 to $5; you should call ahead to check with the registrar to determine if there is any fee. (People in a hurry can take a chance and send a few dollars as a precaution.)

With transcripts in hand, you can get a rough idea of what college credits you'll be able to transfer by understanding the restrictions discussed in Chapter 5. Next, review all the credit-building methods in the previous chapters. The purpose of this second read-through is to separate the methods into yes, no, and maybe categories. Criteria for evaluating credit-building techniques vary according to individual needs, but the following ten questions can help you form evaluation guidelines. Then, as you review each method, you can begin differentiating them for your use.

THE WAITING GAME

At this stage of the process, you'll begin working directly with schools and their administrators. As a result, you'll probably begin to experience delays and lost requests. This is meant as a word of warning so you can plan for these problems as well as limit your exposure to them. Nothing is worse than to ask for information or help from a school, wait for weeks, and then find out that your request was misplaced. It doesn't happen all the time, of course, but it does occur often enough to warrant an alert. Many times in the process of doing research for this book I would make a call to a school where the phone went unanswered. Also, keep in mind that most schools curtail operations during traditional school breaks and summer session.

Exploratory Questions for Credit-Building Preferences

1. How important is it for you to find a low-cost way to earn credit?
2. How important is it for you to finish your degree quickly?
3. Which phrase best describes your independent study capability?
    a. I require plenty of external motivation.
    b. I can motivate myself reasonably well.
    c. I am most productive when left alone to plan and complete studies.
4. How much unquestionable college-level learning do you possess right now? How much of that learning occurred outside the classroom?
5. Are you more interested in completing a degree or having a quality learning experience? If not of equal interest, how much do you prefer one over the other?
6. How many hours per week could you apply to courses and study?
7. Does work travel (or other personal circumstance) prevent you from completing coursework that requires finished assignments at fixed times?
8. Do you have the equipment (computer, printer, modem, VCR, cable TV, etc.) to use emerging educational options?
9. Review any training, certificates, and military experience that you have received. How much of it do you think might be worth college credit?
10. In general, when facing exams and tests you feel:
    a. dread, fear, and the feeling you can't do well.
    b. calm if prepared, a little anxious if not.
    c. ready to triumph.

Consider these questions as a way to profile yourself. With this perspective, look again at each credit-building method and choose (with some objectivity) key methods that are appropriate for you. As you go through the credit-building methods, classify the methods by listing them as yes, no, and maybe. In the next chapter, this list will assist in the evaluation of colleges and universities, and it will help you find a match between your preferred credit-earning methods and a school that can serve you.

The process of planning your degree is often nothing more than determining what you can and can't do. As with most complex situations, carefully eliminating alternatives makes decisions less difficult. In the next chapter, you'll do more of the same by whittling down the list of potential schools from dozens to just a few.

Credit-Earning Methods	Yes	Maybe	No
Traditional classroom studies			
Transfer credit			
Independent study			
Challenge exams			
Standard exams for college credit			
Prior learning/portfolio assessment			
Company-sponsored education			
Certificates and licenses			
Military credit			
Individualized study			

12

Strengthen Your Degree Plans by Choosing the Right School

After selecting your key credit-building methods, you can consider which school will best accommodate your learning preferences. Appendix B contains information about regionally accredited schools offering valuable degrees to technical professionals (or those interested in becoming technical professionals). However, you need to develop some additional criteria for selection, as well as make a special effort to narrow the list of candidate schools. This chapter will help you decide which schools go on your shortlist, and then will show you how to choose the school where you intend to matriculate. You'll also do research and study of colleges on your shortlist.

Schools can be rated by many characteristics, but college advisors say that people who want technical degrees focus on the following criteria: how long it takes to graduate, and how much it will cost. However, you shouldn't jump to the conclusion that the best degree programs are quick and cheap. Other attributes need to be considered when you make your shortlist of colleges to investigate further.

Survey, Study, and Sift Colleges and Universities

Some people have the time, capability, and inclination to read as much college material as possible and will request information from dozens of schools. This isn't the case for most, so the trick is to identify five or fewer candidate schools. Evaluate the options of schools listed in Appendix B as well as other schools that you find while doing your research. The answers to your self-assessment questions will help you reduce the list of schools to a workable shortlist. After you've done this:

- Contact the schools via letter or telephone.
- Request to receive information concerning the degree(s) you are interested in.

PERSONAL CRITERIA FOR EVALUATING COLLEGES

As in the previous chapter, you should do some self-evaluation. At this point, you want to discover what criteria are important to use as you evaluate schools. The following questions will help you pinpoint characteristics you desire in an adult-oriented institution.

- Is finishing your degree quickly a major concern?
- Do you need to find a low-cost school?
- How important is the reputation of the school?
- What size school would suit your needs?
- Do you require an external college? If not, what is the maximum amount of travel to school (frequency and distance) that is acceptable to you?
- Are you looking for an individualized degree program?
- What primary credit-building methods do you want to use? How strongly do you feel about your chosen credit-building methods?

Colleges will respond by sending out (at their expense) catalogs, bulletins, handbooks, and other promotional materials. Some colleges send out a teaser brochure that asks you to request a catalog; sometimes they require you to buy it for a few dollars.

Remember, schools can't exist without paying customers (students), so don't ever be intimidated. Many administrative employees at colleges and universities are efficient and helpful, although you may run across someone with an attitude problem, which will require more diligence on your part.

Making Sense of College Materials

Once you get college materials, you may find reading through them as inspiring and evocative as travel brochures. Colleges are in the business of competing for students, but their typical promotional materials shy away from blatant hucksterism. A common selling point of postsecondary education is that it will open the door of opportunity, which is undeniable. However, be careful to separate the steak from the sizzle as you evaluate each school from its printed material. It isn't enrollment that brings you benefits, it's graduation. The purpose of evaluating colleges is to find one that presents you with the best opportunity to gain the degree you need.

A bit of advice on the school catalogs you'll receive: The range of degree requirements varies widely. In one catalog, you may find the school's requirements are tightly specified and inflexible. At the other end of the spectrum are the liberal, design-your-own-degree schools. Many people find these open programs disorienting and look for another catalog or bulletin containing the degree list. Try to gain a sense of each school's philosophy and determine if you're comfortable with it. When you get comfortable, start looking at the specific degree requirements.

You should be looking at the materials to identify one to five finalists for your shortlist; better yet, try for three or fewer. Details of degree programs, costs, enrollment restrictions, and requirements vary widely from school to school, as does the terminology used to describe programs. If you become confused or have questions, don't be afraid to contact schools to ask as many questions as necessary. Another good reason to contact advisors: They're often the quickest route to other information not usually included in promotional materials, such as the success rates of recently matriculated students. Rely on advisors to add clarity to the information presented in the printed materials and to answer further questions as you refine your criteria and narrow your selections.

TIPS WHEN CONTACTING COLLEGES AND UNIVERSITIES

- Always try to establish contact with the proper department (e.g., external degrees, adult degrees, independent study, etc.) It's even better if you have specific person to contact. Call first to establish contact and to get names, department numbers, and the catalog price (if applicable). A short call can prevent delays in getting the right materials.

- Be specific in stating your reason for contact. A good example of what to say: "I'm researching colleges and universities for possible enrollment in a baccalaureate degree program in information sciences. I need information, bulletins, applications, and catalogs sent to me, as well as an advisor's name." If you are looking into a special program such as an external degree, mention this as well.

- Include day and evening phone numbers and the best time to call you. Keep in mind that not all schools will be in your time zone. Include your full address on all correspondence (both letter and envelope).

- Most schools have many departments. These departments can be so fragmented and isolated from each other that it may take some probing to discover the right one to contact. The nontraditional departments are often small and obscure. If you feel you're

continued on next page

Shortening the List

As you review degree programs, consider the types of credit required to graduate. A concern of many adult students is the amount of mathematics required. This may seem like a tough requirement to avoid with technical degrees, but some schools require less math than others. Keep in mind that by scrutinizing individual degree programs, you may uncover one that specifies credit requirements matching your capabilities.

Residency requirements are a major consideration, and there is a whole spectrum of offerings, from 100 percent external study to years of required on-campus coursework. Intermediate options are becoming more popular; for example, many schools permit most of the work to be done off-campus but hold regular sessions for group communication. These short-residency, on-campus sessions may be held at varying intervals ranging from once a week to a few times a year. In general, the closer to 100 percent external a degree program is the more consideration you can give it without regard to your own proximity to campus. Likewise, the more a degree requires on-campus work, the closer the school must be to your home. Also, in general, external degrees tend to cost less than residency required programs, although there is an adjustment for out-of-state tuition.

Match Your School to Your Key Credit-Building Methods

Schools also discover the individual credit-building methods that are right for them. No school is equipped to evaluate all the methods of earning credit; in fact, among the accepted methods, some are strongly preferred. Some examples of preferred method mixes are:

- Standardized exams and independent study
- Independent study and prior learning
- Individualized study and traditional coursework

Transfer credit is available for use in almost every degree program, no matter what methods are preferred. In technical degree programs, keep an eye on requirements for lab courses; these credits can be particularly hard to earn outside the classroom. Looking for programs with the fewest lab requirements is one way to increase your flexibility when completing degree coursework.

Within the credit-building descriptions, there are various constraints on use—for example, the course age limits on transfer credit. For each preferred credit-building method, you should understand these constraints and gauge each school appropriately.

continued from previous page

not getting the right information, talk to an administrator. Otherwise, you could end up with the same college materials sent out to high school seniors. When you make a follow-up call, remember that the person who answers the phone will most likely be a low-level employee or a student, so try to get transferred to a higher-level employee or administrator.

RUTHLESS ELIMINATION

Don't be afraid to eliminate schools if you find others that look better. One student found a school that was about right, but discovered the school didn't offer portfolio assessment; instead it required a special assessment at which he had to appear in person. He says,

"That means paying the travel costs and the assessment fee. It was scary that it was all hinging on the oral assessment with no guarantee, so I looked at the schools offering portfolio analysis and said 'Hey, here's another way to do it.'"

This student eventually graduated, earning nearly 30 semester credits with portfolio assessments.

School Size and Other Measures

School size can sometimes be a factor, but it's important to realize that, first, there's no agreed-upon size measurement that can be applied evenly across the board and, second, bigger isn't always better. Student population is a suitable yardstick if it measures only the nontraditional enrollment. It isn't unusual to find a small nontraditional degree program (fewer than 100 enrolled students) within the realm of a much larger traditional institution.

Another size measurement that may prove useful is the average number of graduates per year. Also, the number of graduates with technical degrees could indicate the type of support and experience a school puts behind high-technology students. As you collect further information, the dropout rate (and reasons for dropping out) is also useful (though perhaps difficult to come across).

Regarding size, be wary of enrolling in a stepchild degree program. An example of this is a school that offers a technical degree that has graduated only a handful of students. Many schools keep these degree programs open to offer a full range of options, but they emphasize other majors (such as business or liberal arts). This type of school may not be fully able to support you if you need assistance. Look at the number of graduates in your field as an indicator of how well you'll be supported by a school should you enroll.

Look for Majors and Degrees You Want

If you've set your goals and determined which degree (or degrees) you need, you have another way to narrow the list of schools to give further consideration. Don't always require an exact match when looking at degrees offered; not all schools use the same name for equivalent degrees. One example of this is computer software, an area in which you might be interested in any of the following degrees.

- Computer science
- Information systems
- Computers and information systems
- Computer software
- Computer engineering
- Software engineering
- Management information systems
- Business data processing

Also, look for degrees that have generic names (such as engineering or systems engineering) that can be customized (through core and elective credits) into exactly the study program you want.

THE BIG REVELATION

At one orientation session for an individualized program, a school representative explained that participating students set up their own degree programs. Apparently this concept took a while to sink in, but then someone asked incredulously, "A minute ago, you said that I could study what I wanted to. What was it you really meant?" After being told that what was said was what was meant, a realization hit the person, who exclaimed, "You mean I can study what I want to study?"

Another degree option discussed in the credit-building chapters is the individualized degree program. One way to tell if an individualized degree program is right for you is if you can be described with many of the following adjectives: curious, intuitive, risk-taking, passionate, caring, stubborn, self-determined, dedicated, and entrepreneurial.

Individualized study is an exact fit for someone who has a pent-up, righteous desire to study an area not covered by traditional programs (or not covered in enough depth). If this sounds like your situation, this could be another degree type to add to your list as you search for schools.

Individualized (or open) programs have inherent appeal, but only a small percentage of students are truly suited to them. The administrative and preparation hurdles are significant, plus individualized degree programs are small—total enrollment (at each school) often is in the tens to low hundreds. Still, graduates of such programs do better in obtaining direct employment in the area of their degrees; this is probably an indicator of how the passion that drove their study carried over into the job search.

If you plan on getting more than one technical degree (for example, first a BS and then an MS in electrical engineering) it's wise to consider whether the first degree increases or decreases your chance of being accepted to a graduate program at a different school. Some traditional graduate schools have standards that, in effect, eliminate students that graduate from certain schools. (This policy affects graduates of traditional and nontraditional schools alike.)

When you identify your shortlist of undergraduate school candidates, call colleges that you would eventually like to be admitted to for graduate work to ask if they accept graduates from schools you are considering, or if they have any restrictions that would make it hard to get in with degrees from those schools. To avoid disappointment, do this investigation before you matriculate in your first degree program. (Also, see Appendix C to understand the importance of specialized accreditation.)

Evaluating Degree Cost

Degree cost is tricky to ascertain. The first problem is that you don't know the exact amount of credit you need until you matriculate with a school and go through its initial evaluation. Certain schools are willing to do some degree of preevaluation, but for obvious reasons the amount they can do is limited. However, if you're concerned with categorizing schools as inexpensive, moderate, or expensive, using the self-evaluation method

**MILITARY
IN-STATE STATUS**

Active military personnel are often considered in-state residents no matter where they're stationed; check individual policies at each school. Also, active military personnel are considered eligible for some external degree programs that might otherwise be limited to in-state residents.

recommended in the previous chapter (the amount of core technical credits needed plus the amount of general education credits needed) may serve that purpose.

Costs for completing college fall into three major areas.

1. Fees for services
2. Tuition fees for college credits
3. Books

Fees for services start at enrollment and end at graduation (yes, there is a fee to graduate). Costs for credits are usually billed by the credit hour, though some colleges use methods such as a lump-sum charge for an entire quarter. The real way to evaluate cost is to read each college's fee schedule (it may be in the catalog or appear on a separate form). Start adding the charges you would expect to incur for your degree program. Take a close look at how transfer and exam credit is evaluated. Many schools include it as part of the initial enrollment or yearly maintenance fee; others make no cost distinction between transfer credit and classroom-based credit (this practice is regarded by some as gouging the student). Another basis of tuition charges is for the school to charge a flat rate for either full- or part-time attendance by the quarter or semester.

Look also for differences between in-state and out-of-state fees. External colleges (and colleges with minimal residency requirements) don't usually bump their fees by much for out-of-state students. For your ideal program, the difference in fees may not be enough to discourage you, but this area can create unpleasant surprises after you matriculate. These increased costs usually take the form of higher tuition costs.

If you have an educational benefit from your employer, costs should be evaluated against what your company will cover. Policies are different from company to company and sometimes differ by job title. Technology industries are usually among the most progressive in the area of educational benefits, but be sure to check your company's policies. Some of the typical costs that are reimbursed may include tuition, fees, books, special exams, travel, and parking. Payment may be based on the final grade. The best payment program is one that doesn't reimburse you, but instead gives you the money in advance. However, if you don't pass, some companies ask for their money back.

To understand the range of costs to complete a college degree, it's helpful to look at both low-cost and high-priced options. For this example, a hypothetical student is considering a bachelor's technology degree and has two years of college completed (60 credits earned, 60 needed to graduate). In the low-cost approach,

FREE/CHEAP FINANCIAL AID INFORMATION

You can access information about college and financial aid through the following resources.

- The federal government provides various forms of financial aid; this information is presented in *The Student Guide to Federal Financial Aid Programs*. To obtain a free copy, call 1 (800) 433-3424.
- For a basic understanding of how financial aid works, look for a College Board publication *Meeting College Costs*. A high school guidance office should have a copy for you to review.
- *Need a Lift?*, an annual publication of the American Legion, contains career and scholarship information. Single copies may be obtained without charge by calling (317) 635-8411.

continued on next page

the student uses exams and other inexpensive methods; in the high-priced approach, the student uses an expensive fast-track school with plenty of classroom study.

College Degree Costs

Low-End Degree Costs:

Enrollment fees	
First year	$250
Second year	250
Graduation	50
Tuition costs per credit hour (all in-state)	
30 hours of exams	$180
15 hours portfolio assessment	150
15 hours of community college	300
Books	
Total used/borrowed materials	$125
Low-end degree total	$1,305

High-End Degree Costs:

Enrollment fees	
First year	$350
Second year	150
Third year	175
Graduation	250
Tuition costs per credit hour (all in-state)	
60 hours of coursework	$14,000
Books	
Total new materials	$2,225
High-end degree total	$17,150

Financial Aid: The Basics

No look at the cost of college would be complete without mentioning financial aid. Since financial aid is the subject of many other books, this discussion will focus on the subject as it applies to nontraditional schools and technical professionals considering reentering school after a long break.

The process of obtaining financial aid for college, including nontraditional institutions, has changed in the last 25 years. Scholarships used to be awarded primarily for academic excellence, with some awards going to those in true financial need; now eligibility for most aid depends solely on need. The spirit of equity is alive in this new era, but costs at colleges and universities have skyrocketed, which leaves those in normal circumstances in a bind.

continued from previous page

- Every state administers financial aid programs; contact your state's departments of education for more information. States are often the source of scholarships and grants.
- High school guidance counselors keep plenty of guides on hand for their students; if you make arrangements, you can look at these materials, and you may also be able to get some personal help from the counselors.
- Some student-aid programs are designed to assist specific groups *Higher Education Opportunities for Minorities and Women* is a guide to this type of assistance published by the U.S. Department of Education. You can find it in most libraries and high school guidance offices. It may also be purchased; call the U.S. Government Printing Office at (202) 783-3238 for ordering information.

Fortunately, the nontraditional approach can make the process of obtaining your degree less expensive than a traditional education. (An expensive nontraditional school may be equivalent in cost to a mid-range traditional school.) The point here: You can consider the lower cost of these degree alternatives a form of financial aid.

Most people consider higher education an investment. The resulting higher salaries proves it's a wise investment, especially in technology careers. In general, nontraditional schools are supporting part-time adult students, so there's usually not a wide range of financial aid instruments and services for a full-time student to take advantage of. Right or wrong, there seems to be an assumption that these adults will be able to afford the cost of education. Another factor to consider: Many financial aid sources require full-time attendance.

A major source of financial aid is loans. These can be government-guaranteed student loans (usually arranged through a credit union or bank) or the newest instrument of school financing, the credit card (most schools now accept Visa and MasterCard).

Scholarships are available at certain colleges, but there are very few free rides for working adult students. State and federal grants are available as well as veterans benefits. Work-study is a source of financial aid where the student is employed by the school; the work offsets a portion of the college expenses.

Don't forget your employer as significant source of financial aid—take advantage of any existing tuition reimbursement programs. Too many people refuse to do this because they don't want to owe their company anything, but remember: Many high-paid executives have advanced degrees that were paid for by their companies. At a company without a tuition program, try asking for assistance. For courses directly applicable to your work, your manager may have discretionary funds to cover the costs.

Another sad circumstance is when companies offer educational benefits that employees don't use because they don't know about them. Even if you've never heard of these benefits being offered at your company, check with your human resources or personnel department.

Any student can usually find a way to accomplish educational goals if the desire is there, even when the money isn't. Look at financial ability as the convergence of two items.

1. The selection of an appropriate school (regarding cost)
2. A package of financial aid that can sustain your work toward degree completion

BABYSITTING THE BUREAUCRACY

A computer professional relating her experience choosing a school and the process of degree completion says,

"You're dealing with an extremely bureaucratic organization, so with a point of contact you're much further ahead. You get the answers and you put the pieces of the puzzle together, but having someone to assist is extremely helpful."

When you assess how much a school costs, remember this rule of thumb: More expensive schools are more likely to offer you a better financial aid package, so don't count them out right away.

When you think about financial aid, keep in mind that the process of obtaining a complete financial aid package can take up to a year. There are many forms to fill out, including some that ask questions about your financial status. In some cases, you'll need to look for the funds before you identify which school you want to attend.

School Selection: The Final Cut

Next comes the heart of selecting a college with which to matriculate. At this point, you have reviewed a handful of selected colleges and their respective degree programs (as described in their various promotional materials). It's usually to your benefit to not make assumptions about any of the information you read. Going through the materials will help you rereview information and piece together a clearer picture of what you want from a school and degree program. When you begin to get this focus, it's time to further reduce your list of candidate schools. If, after this, you don't end up with a clear winner, then the time has come for comparison shopping.

Published materials from each school only take you to the point where you need to ask specific questions that must be answered by the academic advisors at candidate schools. For instance, an electrical engineering program may state a requirement for lab courses, but what actually qualifies as a lab course? This is the type of area you will want to clarify so you can compare degree programs. When you ask the advisor questions like these, it can make a big difference if you phrase them in the context of your intended degree program. For example, to continue the lab course example, an advisor could be asked to determine how a lab requirement might be met through the use of independent study.

The process of getting your questions answered by advisors should be taken very seriously. Pointed questions, explicit comparisons to other degree programs, student references, and what-if scenarios are all fair game. Again, try to fight any intimidation you may feel (or encounter), because you need to matriculate with the right school. A mistake in choosing your school takes time and money to correct; you must find a better school and start over. The aim in dealing with academic advisors at this point is to acquire all the knowledge you need to make an informed decision. Overall, it's your responsibility to become clear on the what and how of any degree completion path you review. Each school's academic advisor can only provide information and answers.

✓ REDUCE, REUSE, RECYCLE

Once you have selected your school, send postcards to the other colleges and universities asking to be taken off their mailing lists. You'll help reduce the usage of many resources and save everyone a lot of bother, including yourself. Some colleges are extremely aggressive and send out a continuous stream of materials to potential students.

If you come close to making a decision, another call to each of the runner-ups might help cement your decision. If you tell advisors at other colleges why you've chosen to pursue a technical degree at a particular university, they can do one of two things:

1. Concur with your decision
2. Review what they can do for you, and perhaps reveal some better opportunities or benefits if you matriculate with them

This follow-up work is more aggressive than comparing features—you are trying to draw the school into a more competitive mode. Some schools will rise to a competitive challenge while others won't even know a challenge has been made; perhaps each response says something by itself.

Eventually you'll reach a point of diminishing returns when it won't be worth it to get any more information or ask any more questions. If you're going to get a degree, you need to choose a college. It may be tough to make that decision. If so, try this: Go through one more session of reviewing everything you have, and as a last step, make your final determination.

SUMMARY

If you've gone through the steps in this chapter, you've narrowed your list of schools from many to the one that you're planning on applying to. If you've followed the entire process described in this book, you should have:

- Discovered your motivations for wanting a degree
- Identified the degree needed to meet your goals
- Compiled a yes/no/maybe list of credit-building techniques
- Made a decision about which college you will apply to
- Acquired much information about colleges you're no longer interested in

After you decide which school to matriculate with, but before you apply, you'll need to develop your own rough version of a degree plan, including credit-building. This can be considered a degree sketch—your best guess about what credits you already have and what you need to do to complete a degree. In the next chapter, you'll learn what a degree sketch is used for and how to put one together.

13

Create Your Degree Sketch

At this point, if you rush ahead and apply to the college or university that you chose in the last chapter, you presumably will be successful. If so, you'll receive a letter admitting you to the school and matriculating you in the technical degree program of your choice.

This is good news, but if you read this chapter and then prepare a degree sketch, you'll gain a time advantage and realize other benefits as well. A degree sketch will help you better understand what's needed to complete a degree at your chosen school. You can also use the degree sketch to negotiate specifics of that program to your advantage. With a degree sketch, you can begin work on your degree sooner, allowing you to finish earlier. You may also save on certain annual fees—the fee meter starts running when you are accepted.

This chapter will show you how to put together a degree sketch consisting of:

- An inventory of credits you already have
- An inventory of credits you'll need to complete your degree
- How and when you propose to complete the credits needed

What Does a Degree Sketch Look Like?

The following table is a degree sketch developed by Pat, an electronics technician who wants a BS in electronics technology. He has completed approximately two years of college. Having already decided which school to attend, Pat put in about 10 hours (over the course of a week) to develop his sketch. The input to this sketch included:

- His previous college transcripts
- The academic catalog from his chosen school
- Published degree requirements

- A good knowledge of the available credit-building options
- Answers to his questions via phone calls to the school's academic advisors

Sample Degree Sketch:
Bachelor of Science in Electronics Technology

Credit Already Earned:

Arts and Sciences Component

Humanities

Music Theory I (3)
Music Theory II (3)
Trombone 100 Level (3)
Creative Writing (3)

Social Science/History

Colonial America (3)
American History I (3)
Sociology I (3)
Political Science (3)

Natural Science

College Algebra (4)
Calculus I (4)
Zoology (3)
Physics I (3)
Physics II (3)
Linear Algebra (4)

Free Electives

Marketing Principles (3)
Accounting I (3)
Trombone 200 Level (3)
Comparative Literature (3)
Economics (3)
Cultural Anthropology (3)

Electronics Technology Component

Required Courses

Electronics I (3)
Electronics II (3)
Circuit Theory I (4)
Digital Electronics I (3)
Digital Communications (3)
FORTRAN Programming (3)

Electronics Technology
Electives

Digital Process Control (4)
C Programming (3)
Microwave Communication (3)

Credits Needed for Degree Completion:

Complete by month 6:
  Written English: CLEP English Composition/Essay (3)
  Elective: AP Exam in Computer Science (6)
Complete by month 12:
  Technical Writing: Prior Learning Portfolio (3)
  Circuit Theory II: Prior Learning Portfolio (3)
  Systems Design: Prior Learning Portfolio (3)

```
Complete by month 18:
   Elective: Robotics Course, Local College (3)
   Microprocessors: Correspondence Study (3)
Complete by month 24:
   Elective: Measurement Devices, Local College (3)
```

Within the section named Credits Already Earned, note that Pat has listed all past college work in two main categories (Arts and Sciences and Electronic Technology) and then listed each course under subheadings. The main categories and subheadings correspond to those listed in the school's own degree requirements. With this information, Pat can coordinate with an academic advisor after being admitted and then put together an approved degree plan. Bear in mind that the degree sketch is merely Pat's estimate of which credits are applicable.

In the section named Credits Needed for Degree Completion, Pat has listed missing degree requirements and what methods will be used to meet those requirements. Although it's not necessary to show a schedule, Pat does. For example, in the first six months, Pat intends to concentrate on standardized exams to meet a written English requirement, as well as attain some elective credits.

Your degree sketch (like Pat's) will result more from knowledge and information than the process of putting it on paper. This is when you need to untangle college jargon, analyze your selected school's handbook, understand credit-building methods, and imagine yourself as a student. The purpose of this is to develop a proposal of how you plan to complete your degree requirements, and then use your proposal to negotiate an approved degree plan acceptable to both you and your school. The following sections deal with the specifics of how to put together your own degree sketch.

Degree Sketch Format and Content

You can use any format that allows you to both organize your degree sketch and communicate it clearly to an academic advisor. Pat's example sketch is a useful model; it can be adapted. But beware of making the sketch too complex—it's not a report that will be graded. If you don't overestimate the mission of the degree sketch, chances are you'll do the right amount of work. Most academic advisors will be impressed that you've done so much planning. Make the degree sketch a working document: Make it as neat as is practical and skip the pie charts and 3-D bar graphs.

A consideration if you're settled on individualized or open degree programs: The following process needs to be modified because credit-building methods are an integral part of earning the degree. Most of the preparation process is still useful to review, however.

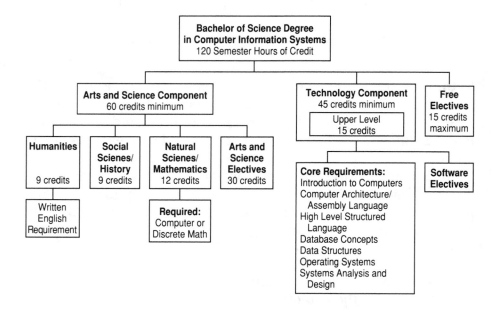

Reprinted with permission from *Technology Degrees* © 1993, The University of the State of New York.

Bachelor of Science in Applied Science and Technology

Credit Distribution Requirements

SUBJECT CATEGORY		Semester Hour Credits
I. Liberal Arts Requirements		**48**
A. Written Expression		6
B. Humanities		9
No more than 6 semester hours may be taken from one subject area		
C. Social Sciences		12
1. Psychology or sociology	(3)	
2. Any selection from anthropology, economics, history, political science, psychology, sociology, or geography.	(9)	
No more than 6 semester hours may be taken from one subject area		
D. Natural Sciences and Mathematics		18
1. College Algebra or above	(6)	
2. General physics or chemistry, depending on specialization	(6)	
3. Additional science or mathematics	(6)	
E. Liberal Arts Electives		3
II. Concentration in Applied Science and Technology		**54**
A. Core Requirements		21
1. Theoretical Knowledge	(12)	
2. Statistics	(3)	
3. Principles of Management	(3)	
4. Technical Report Writing	(3)	
B. Individualized Specialization		33
III. Free Electives		**18**
A. Computer Science or Data Processing	(3)	
B. Free Electives	(15)	
	Total	**120**

Reprinted with permission from *1991–1993 Catalog* © 1991, Thomas Edison State College.

Mechanical Engineering Master's Degree Program

Introduction

In mechanical engineering a student may earn a Master of Engineering (M.E.) degree.

Admission Requirements

Admission to the College of Graduate Studies is open to any student who holds a baccalaureate degree and who presents a scholastic record indicating probable success in graduate work. Generally, an undergraduate GPA of at least 2.8 is required. Admission to the Mechanical Engineering Graduate Program is open to any student with the above qualifications if his or her baccalaureate degree is with a major in mechanical engineering from an ABET accredited program.

Deficiency Courses

Students with a B.S. degree from an accredited engineering program with a major in other closely related disciplines may also be admitted to the Mechanical Engineering Graduate Program. However, such students must demonstrate a proficiency in the subjects included in the BSME program. This generally requires the student to include courses, in addition to the 30 credits of graduate courses required for the Master's degree, which are assigned as a part of the student's study plan as undergraduate deficiencies. The subjects included in the following list define the areas for which proficiency is expected as an entrance requirement for a Master's degree in Mechanical Engineering.

Math   200   Analytic Geometry and Calculus III
Math   310   Ordinary Differential Equations
Math beyond Ordinary Differential Equations
EE   207   Introduction to Electrical Engineering
EE   210   Statics
EE   220   Dynamics
EE   320   Fluid Mechanics
ES   321   Thermo and Heat Transfer
ES   340   Mechanics of Materials
ME   223   Mechanical Design Analysis
ME   261   Engineering Materials
ME   345   Heat Transfer
ME   425   Mechanical Design

Students with a B.S. degree in Mechanical Engineering or closely related engineering disciplines from nonaccredited programs and from foreign universities will also be considered to be admitted to the Mechanical Engineering Graduate Program. If admitted, they will be required to include additional courses as undergraduate deficiencies where their preparation is inadequate and/or does not include the courses previously outlined.

Each applicant to the program is evaluated individually which, on occasion, leads to exceptions and/or substitutions to the above requirements.

Master of Engineering in Mechanical Engineering—Degree Requirements

Area	Level**	Credits
ME 540, Continuum Mechanics	500	3
Mathematics/Statistics/Numerical Methods*	400/500	3
Electives Mechanical Engineering	400/500	12
Mechanical Engineering or other appropriate departments	400/500	12

*That is, classes where this is the primary focus.

Comprehensive Examination: One or two hour oral possibly followed by a written examination on course work.

** At least 18 credits must be at the 500 level.

Examples of Technical Degree Credit Requirements

Reprinted with permission from *Video Outreach Handbook* © 1992, University of Idaho.

Create a Credit Inventory Form

This is more complicated than gathering college transcripts and totaling the credits. You need a list of completed credits that shows how they meet specified degree requirements. Examples of various degree requirements are shown in the illustration, Examples of Technical Degree Credit Requirements. You should think of degree requirements as either subject area categories or specified courses. Examples of subject areas include natural sciences, core technology study, and social sciences; within these subject areas, each degree will specify a certain number of credits needed. An example of a specific course requirement is college English composition.

Start your inventory of completed college credits by copying subject area headings on a sheet of paper; use the subject headings directly from the published requirements for your selected degree program. Organize your headings, leaving space under each. Then add to your list the specific course requirements in your degree program, which will also come from your school's degree requirements. As your degree sketch is developed further, use anything from a pencil to a word processing program to aid in modifications and edits.

Inventory Your Existing College Credits

After you've created the inventory form, get out your college transcripts and list each course under its appropriate heading. Occasionally, it can be a puzzle to figure out where certain courses should be placed on the form. For example, is anthropology a social science or a natural science? Another dilemma occurs when credits that you've already earned don't seem to fit into the degree program you've selected. However, don't panic, even marketing courses can be used in an engineering degree. The following list will help you identify where various liberal art and science courses should be placed.

- **Humanities**: writing, foreign languages, art, music, philosophy, literature, theology, and linguistics
- **Social Sciences/History**: sociology, economics, history, psychology, political science, and cultural anthropology
- **Natural Science**: biology, physics, chemistry, calculus, geology, earth science, astronomy, geometry, and physical anthropology

Compare Your Credit Inventory to Degree Requirements

A simple procedure to use is to go down the list of degree requirements, one item at a time, to see how each corresponding item on your credit inventory measures up. In degree areas where you need more college credit, write down each of these subject areas (or specific courses) and the amount of additional credit required. When you've gone through the entire list of requirements, you should have your first indication of what it will take to finish your degree. (Of course, some refinement is needed at this stage.)

In building a degree sketch, give yourself a little license to aggressively interpret how your credits match up with requirements—that is, when in doubt, show the credit as a match. As you work out the final plan with an academic advisor, you'll participate in determining how your credits match up with degree requirements. For now (and to set yourself up for negotiation), it's best to use an aggressive approach. For example, if your degree requires one computer science/software language course, then match up that requirement with any programming course you have, even if it's an applied type of class. For written English requirements, use any course that required you to learn and demonstrate composition, for example, expository writing, creative writing, argumentative writing, and English composition. Any of these may meet the requirement.

How to Meet Elective Requirements

An often-misunderstood area is the elective component. It's not meant as a catchall for extraneous credits. In technical degree programs, there are usually two types of electives: free and core. Core elective credits can only be fulfilled by courses in the main area of study. Most colleges are still flexible, to the point of including lists of example core courses or special study areas that will apply. With free elective types, students with plenty of transfer credits can fit in credits for unclassified courses such as business.

Another way to meet elective requirements is to use credits you already have that exceed other degree requirements and are "looking for a home." In most degree programs, free elective credits may be met with almost any course; there's typically no expectation that elective credits fit any pattern of usage. A student with specific and aggressive educational goals would likely be more conscientious about using electives to pursue in-depth study of certain subjects.

Lab Course Requirements

Many technology degrees have a requirement for courses with a laboratory component. The best way to determine what existing credits had a lab component is to review course descriptions. To obtain course descriptions for your classes, contact the registrar at each college you attended. Ask for all course descriptions from the time you registered. A description usually tells whether the class had a lab component. If you think the descriptions sent to you are wrong or incomplete (it has happened), ask the registrar to probe further. Digging on your own, you might find old syllabi, lab notes, or laboratory texts that can support your contention that a class did indeed have a lab component. This is proof that you can submit to a transcript evaluator.

Rearrange Your Credit Inventory for Maximum Usage

The next step in the inventory is to move courses around on your inventory form in order to maximize credit for the courses you've already completed.

What happens to credits that exceed even the elective areas? This is a good question to ask a college advisor, so don't give up on the credits. There may be a way to apply them that you don't see; if not, they will be lost—that is, not applicable toward your degree requirements. This is a common occurrence, especially when a student has a large patchwork of existing credits or when credits were earned with a radically different degree program.

The main point about developing this part of the degree sketch: There's more than one way to structure it. It should be structured in line with your needs. Degree requirements are somewhat vague, so don't be bashful about putting forward your own aggressive interpretation of degree requirements—it may be legitimate. The degree sketch is a negotiating tool by which you will arrive at a final degree plan with your school.

Match Up Inventory and Degree Requirements to Get Credit Where Due

Taking the process to this point completes the credit inventory and helps you identify where credits will need to be earned. Now you must go back to your specific degree requirements and compare them to your inventory. With this comparison, you'll find what credits are needed to finish a degree.

No matter how your degree sketch has turned out, remember that as a nontraditional student you have options other than full-time classroom study. Part of the purpose of the degree sketch is to help you find ways to earn those remaining credits according to your abilities.

Identify Credit-Building Methods

The next objective in developing your degree sketch is to evaluate credit-building options with respect to the list of credits needed to

WRITTEN ENGLISH REQUIREMENTS

A point to keep in mind for the nearly universal written English requirement: No matter which method you use, when you present your degree plan, make sure it's clear how you intend to complete (if necessary) this requirement. A common mistake is assuming that any English course will satisfy the requirement.

graduate. This can be a complex process, but is simpler if you've already:

- Chosen your own key credit-building options
- Studied your degree program requirements
- Itemized credits needed to finish your program

The first item involves applying your selected credit-building methods, and the second and third items are accomplished by working the degree sketch through to this point.

Organize your list of required credits and write them down. Now go down the list, item by item, and think about how you can meet those degree requirements. Ideally, you're going to think first about using the key credit-building methods you've selected.

If, for example, your list includes 12 credits to be earned in electronics and you've selected independent study as a key credit-building method, this is the time to look at various sources for electronics independent study courses and see what's offered (you can use Peterson's Guide or other sources). If you have history electives that need to be met and you've favored standardized exams, you'll find what you need by exploring history exams offered by CLEP, ACT PEP, and others.

There's an endless combination of ways to earn the credits you need to graduate. Stick with the primary credit-building methods and you'll be able to quickly move forward with your degree sketch. Another technique that helps you match credits needed with a specific way to earn them is to view the list of credits needed in one of two categories: required courses and elective blocks of credit. Some nontraditional credit-building methods tend to mimic traditional classroom study (credit gets earned in a specific course), while others permit larger awards of credit in wider areas of study (a better fit for elective credits). To prevent entanglements, identify credit-building methods for specific courses first, then work on the blocks of elective credits.

Understanding how each method is used and where opportunities exist is critical to optimizing your degree plan. Otherwise, you might find yourself overusing traditional methods. Credit-building opportunities may be explored using this book and the additional resources listed, but as with college selection, ask an academic advisor to guide you when developing your degree sketch. If you find your selection of credit-building methods is tangled or drifting toward unwanted classroom study, contact an advisor for assistance. In this portion of the degree sketch, rely on the use of your chosen key credit-building methods, but fall back on others where necessary.

A Timetable for Completion

The college or university where you matriculate is usually not concerned with the time it takes you to finish your degree. There are sometimes maximum time limits, but these are usually not a concern in an adequately executed degree plan. This portion of a degree sketch is useful for establishing goals for completion; with it you can see how degree work meshes with your other responsibilities and eliminate conflicts within the degree sketch itself. When complete, it also serves as a way for you to measure your own performance, without which your efforts may stall. There are several ways to estimate degree program completion; the recommended one uses levels of refinement to produce an achievable schedule integrating desire and capability.

To start, build a timetable without reference to a calendar—only define credit-completion goals at the end of six-month periods. A period shorter than six months is too detailed for this degree sketch, and a longer period (such as a year) is too loose to track progress. A chronological list is a sufficient planning tool (as shown in the earlier example), but a timeline, calendar, GANTT chart, or other method can be used as well. However the schedule is conveyed, it must communicate when portfolios, exams, other evaluations, and coursework will result in an expected credit award for specific degree requirements.

Give some thought to the order of credit-building. Arranging it in ascending order of difficulty makes sense, especially if credits are needed in a study series (for example, Calculus I followed by Calculus II). Another way to order is by getting easier credits out of the way. Some people are inspired by making headway early in the process. For instance, easy CLEP exams are a good choice for earning early credits. On the other hand, some choose to pursue the toughest portions of their credit-earning earliest, with the notion that if the degree plan has flaws, it's better to discover them early for more flexibility in adjustment. Play with the credit-building order until it fits and feels right to you.

Take a Second Look at Your Degree Sketch and Schedule

To avoid overcommitting yourself, compare your initial completion timetable and the work required during each six-month period. To help you estimate individual credit-completion efforts, use the credit-building methods described in previous chapters as well as associated materials such as exam descriptions, course syllabi, and orientations. Also, advisors can be of great assistance because they have helped students with similar needs. In going back to refine the completion timetable, you don't have to stretch

An interesting pattern seen repeatedly: When one adult achieves a nontraditional degree, it often inspires another adult in the family to evaluate his or her situation and eventually pursue a degree.

out the schedule, but instead may find that you can be a little more aggressive. Don't spend too much time refining. Chances are you've probably come close; only look for estimates that are way off.

Match Your Completion Schedule to Other Schedules

It's time to get out the calendar and map your completion timetable against what happens in the real world. Regarding time, so far you've only considered personal consequences. The time availability of credit-building methods should be considered. For example, classroom courses and exams aren't offered on demand, so you must research to make sure the timing matches your sketch; otherwise, adjustment will be necessary.

Some schools can't provide a schedule beyond their immediate offerings; in this case, the best technique is to spread out your plans for classroom study over time. Your schedule then allows for the fact that the school won't offer all the courses you need at once. Also remember that exams are scheduled at certain times of the year—sometimes only once a year—so plan accordingly.

Stay on Schedule with Time-Management Techniques

An important aspect of any completion timetable is a balanced, sustainable study plan. A number of simple practices help guide the creation of study plans, and are also wise study habits. The brief treatment given them here isn't meant to convey a lack of importance: A solid study plan contributes greatly to successful credit-building.

- For every three credit hours attempted, plan on 10 to 12 hours of study per week.
- Using a chart that shows all waking hours of one week, indicate all activities.
- On your chart, place study blocks in one to two hour increments. Find enough blocks to satisfy the 10-to-12-hours rule.
- Set up a regular place to study as free from distractions as possible.
- Enter each study block with a plan of what needs to be covered.
- Maintain some flexibility in your studying. Adjust to cope with increased or decreased needs.

Few people have uncommitted hours that they can dedicate each day to new endeavors. Whether they realize it or not, most adult students face a classic time-management problem. Many books have been written on the subject of getting more out of your time (as well as better study habits). The following is a brief summary of basic time-management axioms for adult students.

- Simply trying to do more will not work.
- Something must be given up or cut back.
- Creativity can expand the time available.

The first axiom is based on the premise that you aren't sitting around waiting for something to happen in your life. In fact, the opposite is true for most nontraditional students: The same drive that propels them toward attaining educational credentials has driven them to have full lives.

The second axiom is the logical progression from the first, but is far from a desperate statement. Relief must be sought, and it comes in many forms. Employers often get behind an educational plan and make such accommodating arrangements as:

- Relieving you of a few work responsibilities
- Accepting a slightly reduced workday
- Granting occasional leaves of absence or unpaid time off
- Granting occasional paid time off with no strings attached
- Granting occasional paid time off with some strings (for example, a contract for employment beyond graduation)
- Permitting you to combine work and study into a project
- In high-tech professions, letting you work a 40-hour work-week (instead of the usual "50-hour" 40-hour workweek)

The level of accommodation depends on the culture of your company, your supervisor, and your own standing within the company. If your employer cooperates, it's important to stay within the bounds of any agreement or custom. Abuse of any consideration or slipping work performance may draw scrutiny. Remember, the company may not only withdraw your support, it may refuse similar support to others in the future.

For those with families and/or strong friendships, this can be a time of cooperation. Degree costs can be measured in time and money, but the basis for motivation is often rooted in the indirect enhancement of family life (e.g., more job security and a promotion). Many people are supported by the help they receive from their family and friends. This means that you may be able to share your responsibilities with people around you so that you can pursue your goal.

The third axiom is not meant to imply that the first can be voided. Perhaps it should be altered to read "Creativity can expand the time available by a small amount." Examples of creativity: combining study with other activities or trying different approaches to current activities. Some typical combinations include studying

DRIVER TRAINING

A nontraditional student in the traffic-congested New York/New Jersey area uses a cassette player in the car to get the most out of the daily trip to work:

"Each day I have two 60-mile commutes and I've learned to turn that into a valuable study time. I tape the audio portion of a video course or I recite chapters from a textbook into the recorder. Then I play them over and over in my car, and the more I hear that material, the more I retain."

and reading during lunch, and skimming texts or study guides during TV commercials (if you must watch TV). Methods such as listening to tapes while you sleep seem to cross over the line of sensibility, however.

Another example of creativity in time management is to cut down on wasted time. For example, some people maintain cardiovascular fitness by regularly attending health clubs. Good health is probably the most important thing you can have (yes, even more important than a college degree), so maintaining an exercise program is good common sense. However, if using a health club takes up too much time, you might want to consider setting up exercise equipment at home.

Calculating Cost

The final part of the degree sketch is looking at how much it will cost. Even if your employer pays 100 percent of your school costs, you still have to cover some expenses until you're reimbursed after completing the course. If you're paying the bill yourself, estimating the costs of the degree is important. The following are types of expenses that you may incur while pursuing a nontraditional degree.

- Registration fees
- Annual enrollment fee
- Transfer evaluation fees
- Examination fees
- Prior learning or other evaluation fees
- Course tuition
- Textbooks and study guides
- Supplies and lab costs
- Proctoring fees
- Travel expenses (including fuel and parking)
- Extra childcare
- Equipment, computers, and calculators
- Graduation fees

If you expect that your income will decline for any period while you're completing the degree, factor this in. (One such scenario is if you're unable to work as much paid overtime as usual). While most people agree that a degree can pay for itself, it still must be paid for up front; however, planning the expenses is relatively easy to do. After you've put together your timetable for completion, compute up front the recurring fees (such as registration and regular enrollment), then add the costs associated with taking your planned courses (tuition, books, and other fees and expenses).

SUMMARY

In this chapter, you've gone through the college-level work you've completed and found out where you need to earn credits. Taking it a step further, you now have an idea about how you can earn the credits as well as when you might be able to complete the degree. The degree sketch is comprised of all this information and will serve you immediately when you work with your academic advisor at the school you've chosen.

The purpose of the degree sketch regarding costs is to help you plan expenses, but another benefit is that you can get a good idea of your likely expenses. If, as a result of this work, you think you can afford a more expensive school (or conversely, find you need to choose a cheaper one), then your degree sketch has proven valuable in yet another way.

14

Get a Head Start
When You're Admitted

Matriculating in a nontraditional college degree program is a process much the same as at traditional colleges: After choosing the school, you apply for admission into a particular college with a chosen degree program. This admissions process is usually a standard procedure that involves completing an application form and arranging to have your high school and college transcripts sent. Depending on the school you select, you might also have to submit a short written essay and/or one or two personal recommendations. As routine as this sounds, you can make the process more efficient and get a quicker, easier approval of your degree plan.

Getting Accepted Is Usually Painless

Getting accepted at an undergraduate nontraditional school is usually not a problem, though nontraditional graduate schools can be more demanding. Even people who didn't do well in high school and college are usually able to gain acceptance to a nontraditional school. The underlying reason for this is that adult students are different and deserve educational alternatives. (If you didn't finish high school, see Appendix D).

Within nontraditional circles, many stories are told of people who return to school as adults and graduate with honors even after dreadful first experiences in higher education. College advisors in technical degree programs see many success stories involving people who initially thought they weren't college material. These advisors often say that older students can accomplish as much in their education as they have in their careers. So be encouraged, but bear in mind that the completion of all nontraditional degree programs is taken very seriously by the schools. All conditions of maintaining active status, including minimum grade levels, are monitored.

There are a few important admission requirements to watch for: residency, age, and time away from a traditional school. Residency usually concerns state residency. There are sometimes minimum age restrictions, usually around 22 to 24 years. To prevent a rush by traditional students to nontraditional schools, certain schools require that a student not have been in good standing at another school for some period of time, usually six months. These and many other restrictions can be waived; if you encounter such restrictions, plan on spending extra time clearing them up during the admission process.

Make the Most of Your Time During the Admission Process

A few colleges allow you to go through a preenrollment evaluation or extensive orientation program. Take advantage of this if possible; enrollment usually constitutes matriculation, and the clock starts running on any annual fee you have paid. In order to save money, learn in advance how to go directly through transfer evaluation and get approval for your degree sketch. Don't wait until you enroll to prepare your materials (including your degree sketch); after-admission preparation time costs come out of your pocket. Two rules that can save time and money are to understand the application and evaluation process, and to work each in parallel as much as possible.

Matriculation is like a contract that spells out what is required to complete a degree. Degree programs change with some regularity, but matriculation freezes those requirements for you. One way to save money on annual fees is to not matriculate in a program, but to acquire credits and take exams as if you were enrolled. When you've done as much as you can outside matriculation, enroll and have your credits transferred. The problem with this technique is that technical degree requirements change, so earning credits before matriculation can be like trying to hit a moving target. Another factor is that all previous courses get older (review course age concerns in Chapter 5). Anyone considering this approach should think twice before pursuing it. For most people, becoming officially enrolled, getting matriculated, and receiving transcript reports showing a steadily approaching graduation are important motivations.

Confirmation of admission can take weeks or months depending on the school; a letter is the usual means of notification. If you are in a hurry, you can ask for an expedited decision, which may cost you an additional fee.

✓ TRANSCRIPT POSTSCRIPTS

If you have accumulated less than one year of previous college-level work, the school to which you are applying may require a high school SAT or ACT score. If you have taken such an exam, it's probably on your high school transcript. If you haven't, you can contact a local high school and make arrangements to take the exam.

When you contact all your former college-level institutions to arrange for transcripts to be sent to the schools to which you are applying, always include the following information: full name, former name, current address, date of birth, dates attended, and Social Security number. If any of your schools have closed or lost records, notify the school to which you are applying.

Some schools may charge a fee to send transcripts. If you are in a hurry, many schools will (for an additional charge) turn your request around in a few days (two weeks is an average minimum).

Your Degree Plan: Seeking Approval

After you've completed your degree sketch and been admitted, you can begin to seek approval for your degree plan. Some schools don't require you to go through a planning and approval process, but the service is available to you if you want it. You should take advantage of this because with individualized degree programs planning is not only required, it defines the degree program itself. Don't feel like a bother to your academic advisor; enrollment and advising fees are meant to pay for this service.

Organize your degree sketch to clearly indicate what credits are already earned (through expected transfer credit, training evaluation, and other methods) and what credits still need to be earned. Use a format like the one in Chapter 13. The format is basic, but useful enough to get through an evaluation by your academic advisor. Whatever format you decide to use, it must serve both you and your advisor as you negotiate what credits the school will put on your transcript and what work remains.

Working with an advisor and/or transcript evaluator, you first must establish what credits can be transferred to your transcript immediately. As you encounter problems, remember that there's an appeal process for you to use. As you appeal transcript decisions, if you're creative in making your case, you can get those credits back.

After you settle your credit transfer, you'll receive an initial transcript and evaluation. At this point, advisors are ready to look at the section of your proposed degree plan that concerns what you need to obtain your chosen degree. Advisors generally aren't concerned with how long you plan to take. They will go over your proposal, review your evaluated transcripts, and determine whether your credit-building approach will complete all requirements. Questions may arise as part of the advisor's evaluation. For instance, if you listed "local college" on your credit-earning plan (as a source of classroom-based courses), the advisor will probably ask, "Which college do you plan to use? Is it regionally accredited?" Be prepared to answer questions like these, and be ready to supply additional information. To speed up this evaluation process, try using a fax machine to submit additional documentation such as course descriptions from college catalogs and updates to your degree plan.

Putting together this part of the degree plan with your school takes time, so be prepared to do some work to get it fully negotiated. Don't be surprised if it takes two to four weeks to turn your sketch into a plan. Failing to satisfy any questions the school might have

STEPS OF A TIME-EFFICIENT ADMISSION

Some colleges won't accept your enrollment fee until an evaluation is done, but for those considering the typical school method (matriculate first, negotiate degree plan second), the following is an example of ordered steps an alert student can execute to maximize time and minimize expenses.

1. Use an advisor prior to enrollment to unofficially refine your degree plan.
2. Gather all information related to evaluation prior to application.
3. Five days before submitting your application, mail out requests to have official documentation (transcripts and course description) sent to your selected school.
4. Send in your application and enrollment fee.
5. Monitor progress of your application by staying in phone contact with the registrar's office.
6. When you receive confirmation of admission, get in touch with your academic advisor and send him/her a completed degree sketch.
7. Work simultaneously with your transcript evaluator and advisor to complete a transcript evaluation and refine your degree sketch into an agreed-upon plan.
8. Stay in touch with both your advisor and transcript evaluator. Don't get lost in their in basket. Demand their attention.
9. Make arrangements for your initial credit-building methods, and begin preparing as soon as you get prior approval for these methods.

means that you have to submit an alternate approach to meeting questioned requirements. As you proceed through the negotiating process, adjust the schedule and cost estimates for your own benefit.

Once you and the advisor agree on all the details, you've done it—you have a degree plan. If possible, get the advisor's approval in writing. Try to preserve all the documentation concerning negotiated points of the plan. This doesn't mean that you have a rock-solid contract with the school, but if questions come up when you apply for graduation, going through the degree plan and how it was negotiated might be enough to get you through any last-minute snags. Still, take a breath and admire your degree plan. All that stands between you and graduation is credit-earning and administrative paperwork with your school.

■ ■ ■

Example: Working Through the Plan

As an advisor reviews your plan, the concern may arise that one or more courses won't satisfy some degree requirement. Suppose you want to use a correspondence course in microprocessors to satisfy a requirement that specifies a lab component. If you've already researched this and know that the course does have such a component, supplying the advisor with a description of the course materials and a syllabus should bypass any concerns he or she has about the lab portion of the requirement. If the course doesn't have a lab component, you might try showing how one of the other courses with a lab demonstrates the same capability.

• • • • •

TOUGH BUT FAIR PRACTICES

A technology graduate looking back on the treatment he received from his school says,

"I disagreed with a couple of calls of whether a course would fit one requirement or not, but I felt comfortable that they questioned courses because that makes me feel my college has people who care—who are insuring the integrity of my degree. And while it may have been a little frustrating to deal with that, it didn't seriously impact anything."

College Agents: Worthwhile or a Hoax?

People who desire college degrees or other educational credentials have always been the target of con artists operating diploma mills (see Appendix C). A new type of enterprise has arisen for the adult student to consider: college agents. These agents operate under the premise that they can assist you in completing higher education, from enrollment to graduation, with any resulting degree being a prelude to "an exciting new career in (fill in the blank)." By now you know that it takes a lot of effort to put together a degree plan. Is an agent a legitimate shortcut?

Agents have an interesting sales technique to promote their business: They hint at affiliations with almost any legitimate, well-known school. Potential customers may associate the school's legitimacy with the agent and conclude that there's some sort of partnership.

People consider agents for the same reason that some pay thousands of dollars for worthless degrees from diploma mills: "Gee, it sounds too good to be true, but if it's true, I'll be a lot better off than I am now."

These agents typically do work no different than that described in this chapter. With help from a college advisor, motivated students will always do a better job than an agent. There are many unsatisfied customers of college agents; in the worst cases, people have spent thousands of dollars to have the agent evaluate their abilities, tempt them with salary potential (after the degree is obtained), and provide help in filling out a legitimate college application. That's where the agent's service usually ends. Agents may back up their fees with a guarantee of college admission, but they couldn't stay in business if they guaranteed anyone a degree.

When agents are involved, colleges and universities see many students who have been successfully coached through the admissions process. After that, the schools are often left with students who don't possess adequate reading, writing, and study skills. Another sad situation: Schools end up with enrolled students who want a better job but lack the realization that it will take more than a wish to complete an extended period of study.

In conclusion, there's probably no school that has utilized an outside agent to assist in finding and enrolling students. The best advice is to direct your own education with the help of academic advisors at your degree-granting school.

SUMMARY

Getting through the admissions process may make you anxious, but the real activities to concentrate on are preparing yourself for a timely admission and planning a smoother negotiating session as you work out your degree plan. After all, the bulk of your work will be spent in the execution of the degree plan (covered in the next chapter).

Getting to Graduation Day Using the Degree Plan

The degree plan identifies work that needs to be accomplished to graduate as well as time intervals for completion. Despite your effort to complete the plan, you can't see years into the future to anticipate every change in events. Ideally, the planning process will take into account expected and likely events. For example, if you knew that your company is moving you across the country in six months, creating a degree plan that involves a local school is probably a mistake.

Lessen the Impact of Changes in Plans

As you use the plan to guide your work toward completion, remember that any plan or set of goals is subject to changing circumstances. Personal and family events such as babies and unexpected health problems may alter your degree plan. Technical employment is subject to rapid and significant changes that can alter the best of plans. In light of changing circumstances, there are three basic types of modifications that students can make.

1. Alter study habits
2. Change the degree plan
3. Suspend work toward the degree

Disregarding the last option, the modifications may be used together to accommodate change. In any case, the intent is to either speed up or slow down the degree program. You may attempt to complete the degree faster because you have more time (due to a layoff, for example), but since slowing down is more likely, you should consider it first.

Once your degree plan is in place and progress has been made, it can be a hard decision to slow down the pace. No matter what your reasons, the trick is to throttle back the right amount. Since learning and thinking are by nature stressful experiences, you should try to reduce stress to an acceptable level.

Taking a break is an option that may be appropriate if used carefully, but there are consequences and risks in letting progress come to a complete halt. First, degree completion is pushed back by a minimum of the length of the break. Also, some people find that getting away from regular studying makes it that much harder to get going again. Overall, your chance of successfully completing your degree is decreased by lengthening the time to graduation. However, if your degree completion program must slow down, take the appropriate action, and do it without guilt. The nontraditional educational experience is intended as an alternative to traditional study methods that offers the promise of being less of a grind. Many colleges permit delays and even offer breaks on enrollment fees if they are given notice. If you need to slow your progress, be sure to notify the school and follow policies if you are dropping courses or withdrawing; it can save many headaches later.

Is it possible to go faster and finish sooner? Yes, and it's not all that unusual. Students often get especially proficient at using certain credit-building methods—exams and portfolio study are good examples of this. In such cases, the student can change the degree plan to include more of the favored methods, thus increasing credit-building efficiency. The rule that applies in this case: Decrease the time to degree completion and you increase your chance of success.

Changing your degree plan typically doesn't require the approval of your college if you plan to slow down or speed up. Giving notice may be to your benefit if you plan to interrupt your studies—ask if the school will suspend fees for that period. When you change your degree plan to modify the methods used to earn credit, consider the changed portion as subject to negotiation and approval.

Doing Well and Meeting Your Goals

Don't dwell on the information concerning delayed progress—concentrate instead on meeting your goals. When you do succeed, reward yourself. People respond well to positive reinforcement; it works just as well when you're the object of the reinforcement. Your bonus may be a vacation, TV, a massage, recreational reading, a party, or anything that feels good and is suited to the accomplishment. I once attended a bonfire party in celebration of completed exams; fuel for the bonfire came from the various course notes and texts.

Some examples of reasons to reward yourself include:

- Finishing your degree sketch
- Gaining admission to the school you chose
- Successfully negotiating a degree plan
- Completing a course assignment
- Completing any course
- Completing an exam (if you studied hard, treat yourself regardless of how well you think you did)
- Finishing a reading assignment
- Receiving your first updated transcript showing results of initial credit-building efforts
- Receiving an A
- Receiving a C
- Receiving any passing grade or exam score
- Changing your standing (such as from Junior to Senior)
- Submitting your graduation application
- Receiving graduation approval
- Graduating and attending commencement

Gradual Steps to Graduation

This section deals with graduating, a reward that isn't bestowed automatically. To start, you must distinguish between graduation and commencement. You graduate by fulfilling all the degree requirements. If you're due to graduate (or have been approved for graduation), the school will invite you to attend a gathering of other graduates; this gathering is called the *commencement*. The cap-and-gown commencement ceremony is closely identified with graduation, but remember that commencement is a party of sorts (although a party with many speeches may not be a party at all).

A belief that many students hold about graduation: Somewhere in the school's bureaucracy, a lone bureaucrat regularly reviews all transcripts to find students who have completed their degree requirements and are now ready to graduate. When this mythical person finds such students, the school mails out their diplomas. In reality, graduation is a process initiated by the student, who will analyze his or her progress and determine when the time is right to apply for graduation. This is partly why students are given transcript updates when credits are recorded.

Graduating is a process, but when the time comes, shouldn't it be a simple formality? Many people have expressed the sentiment, "Getting through school was tough, but don't ask me to go through the graduation process again." This is certainly an exaggeration, but it says a lot about the frustration of having to jump through one more administrative hoop after doing all the real work (earning credits). Understanding the rules of graduation prepares you for the work at hand, as well as making for a smoother transition from student to graduate. You need to understand the graduation process even though you only go through it once per degree.

■ ■ ■

Example: Surprise, You're Done!

To illustrate how unaware a school can be about your status, consider the following true story. After years of work toward a computer science degree, a student contacted his advisor, with whom he was on a first-name basis. The purpose of the contact was to double-check the student's contention that all degree requirements were met. After a few minutes of looking over the transcript, the advisor said with surprise, "You know, you're right, it really looks like you've finished."

• • • • •

Planning ahead is important. When it appears that you are six to eight months from completing all degree requirements, consult the current graduation schedule at your school. If you don't have a schedule, ask your advisor for one. Schools usually schedule graduation two or three times a year so they can focus faculty and other staff on reviewing candidates for graduation, determining who is and isn't going to make it. When you look at the graduation schedule, try to find a graduation date that comes close to your expected completion date. With each graduation date, there are a number of deadlines, but take special note of the deadlines for application and for final submittal of credits for evaluation and recording (on your transcript).

You apply for graduation by filling out a form and enclosing the graduation fee. The fee is charged to evaluate your transcripts. Since most people are still earning credits at the time they apply for graduation, the school will need to know specific information about remaining credits to be earned so it can work around them. The final deadline for submitting transcripts is the date by which credits must be completed and submitted to the registrar. At a traditional school, this deadline refers to final exams and grades from the professors of your courses. Nontraditional schools are looking for any credits that are needed, whether they came from resident study or any of the other credit-building methods.

You should start the ball rolling well before graduation because there will be many tasks to complete. You'll want your advisor to look at your transcript carefully and tell you what it will take to finish. (Ideally, this matches the credit-building you will already have under way.) When you complete all the work associated with credit-building, it may take time to coax those last few grades and exam scores into the registrar's hands.

Even with the most careful planning, you'll want to prepare to take forceful action if the transcript deadline approaches and needed credits are still not recorded on your transcript. An example of this would be if an independent study professor takes too long to grade your final exam. If the transcript deadline is approaching, contacting both the professor and the sponsoring school is warranted. You can speed up the process by using priority mail, the phone, overnight mail, and fax machines. You can also have other people use these methods; school administrators normally make heavy use of the in-basket and regular mail services.

Your urgency to graduate builds as the day comes closer; this is probably where frustration and anxiety begins to take hold. The prospect of waiting until the next scheduled graduation becomes distasteful, as it should. If you have to remain enrolled for six more months, it could cost you another annual fee. Also, the sooner you get your degree, the sooner you will enjoy the goals you set for yourself; it may even mean an immediate promotion and salary increase. So push, ask for help, and do whatever it takes to gain the cooperation of those involved in your graduation.

The graduation process includes planning, chasing administrators, and ultimately, graduating. After you've met the deadlines, the school will evaluate your request to graduate. If everything is in order, it will send a letter notifying you of degree conferral. Congratulations—this means that you've officially graduated. Now it's time to think about that party.

The Big Day: Commencement

The commencement ceremony is the ritual by which the school attempts to drive home this ironic truth: "Guess what? This isn't the end, this is the beginning. Get out, get going, commence!"

This ritual can be so important that it will drive external students to travel thousands of miles to a campus they've never seen before. Yet there are some students who wouldn't travel across town to attend their commencement. Attendance is optional, so you get to make the choice: Go to the commencement, or have a simple diploma ceremony with your mail carrier.

Realize Your Goals:
What to Do After Graduation

Achieve Your Goals Through Self-Promotion

Earning a degree is an accomplishment, but the next step in fulfilling your goals is to put your diploma to work. Remember that the diploma wasn't the goal; you needed it to achieve other goals. To accomplish your desired results, you'll need some self-promotion. When a degree is awarded, it's a private matter between the student and the school. Commencement, graduation announcements, and excited phone calls to family and friends are typical exercises in promotion, but if your goals are more career-oriented, you'll need to get the word out in a different way.

Tell Your Boss

Don't tell your boss about your degree in the hallway. A good approach is to make an appointment with your manager or supervisor. After all, a degree is an important career qualification, so you'll want to announce and discuss it in the appropriate setting. The message you're trying to send is that you've achieved an educational credential that should be acknowledged by the company. The company's acknowledgement can range from a hearty handshake to an immediate promotion; however, it's reasonable to act like you expect treatment like the latter. Perhaps the minimum you want to get across to your boss is that when the next performance review comes around, you want to be given consideration under these new circumstances.

Tell Your Boss' Boss

You may now have credentials that equal or exceed your own supervisor's. By making your accomplishment known to upper management, you may put yourself in the running for higher-level positions. In an ideal world, your immediate boss wouldn't stand in your way or stifle you; however, it does happen. By making your annoucement at a higher level, you're doing a safe amount of self-promotion. If your culture supports meeting formally with your boss' boss, make an appointment; if not, an informal hallway announcement is appropriate.

Tell Your Human Resource Department

First, get the human resource department a copy of your diploma for your employee file. Second, talk with the recruiter in the personnel department. Recruiters need to know about your new educational credentials; otherwise, they may continue to think you lack them. When you keep the recruiter updated, he or she may consider you for positions that are opening up.

Tell Your Coworkers

In addition to conveying your good news upward in the organization, you will want to foster a new respect for yourself among your peers by telling them also. Someday these people may be working for you, or you may be working for them if they get promoted. Announcing your good news can take many forms, including:

- Hanging your diploma in a visible spot in your office
- Having the news put in the company newsletter
- Sending out a memo or e-mail announcement
- Having your boss send out a memo or e-mail announcement
- Throwing a graduation party for yourself
- Making an announcement at a group or department meeting
- Telling people individually
- Wearing a cap and gown to work one day

Let Potential Employers Know

You may have collected a stack of résumé-rejection letters. With degree in hand, now is the time for you to contact all the rejecting companies and let them know that you have a new résumé that highlights that you've completed your degree. Don't forget to contac the network of people you know. Again, these people may think you lack an important degree, and you'll want to make them aware of your changed situation.

Review Your Goals and Monitor Achievements

A degree can change your life overnight. There are many technology companies that give an instant promotion if you complete a particular degree. Still, there are other situations where the results may be a long time coming and require special attention.

 CRASHING

After most endeavors of extended duration and stress, there's usually a period of elation and satisfaction. In some cases, this is followed by a period of aimlessness, depression, or the blues. *Crashing* is another nickname for those who have recently finished their college degrees only to find that there's something missing in their lives. This is most often a temporary side effect while a student readjusts to a more normal life. It's strange to think people can miss stress, but it happens.

If this happens to you, rather than sign up for another degree right away, it might pay to take a break and do some of the things you used to for pleasure and relaxation. It may take some thinking to remember what those activities were, but they'll come back to you.

One phenomenon that often occurs at work is that your boss and coworkers can't think of you in a different way. A common reward for excellent work in tough situations is more work in tough situations. People who lack educational credentials often make themselves so valuable in their current positions that a promotion or other reward seems like a mistake. A manager may not think he or she can replace promoted employees. (After all, who else could do so much work so well for so little money?)

In any situation where you're not achieving desired and expected career improvements, it's always wise to speak up. Talk with your manager, talk with his or her manager, and talk to a human resource representative. At first, it pays to be patient, but if you're unsatisfied, it's important to find (and ask for) specific opportunities. Eventually it may become imperative for you to research changing companies in an attempt to achieve career goals.

In any event, pay attention to the progression of goal realization. It usually takes some nurturing as you go. You want to look back on your educational experience as worthwhile.

Do You Want Another Degree?

Of course, this book is not going to answer this question for you, but the decision-making process is much the same as for degree planning: Set your goals and determine if another degree would help meet them.

Educational credentials aren't everything. Putting what you've learned to use and gaining practical experience may be the best thing to do after earning one degree. Still, many people find the whole experience of earning a degree easy and fun and can't wait to go after another.

The focus of this book has been on nontraditional education. There are many reasons for choosing a nontraditional degree that may not apply your second time around: expediency, time, and cost are just a few. If you decide to go after another degree, it makes sense to carefully weigh the fundamental decision again: Should you choose a traditional or nontraditional route?

Glossary

AARTS: Army/ACE Registry Transcript Service. Provides transcripts of Army training for people who enlisted after 1981.

Accredited: Refers to regional accreditation, meaning that the college or university is accredited by a COPA-recognized agency. For more information, see Appendix C.

ACE: American Council on Education.

ACT PEP: American College Testing Proficiency Examination Program.

Admission: The process by which a student is admitted to an institution for the purposes of enrolling in classes and/or pursuing a particular degree.

AP: Advanced Placement exams.

Associate's Degree: A terminal degree program equivalent to two years of full-time study in designated study areas (approximately 60 semester credits or 90 quarter credits).

Baccalaureate Degree: A terminal degree program equivalent to four years of full-time study in designated study areas (approximately 120 semester credits or 180 quarter credits).

Bachelor's Degree: see Baccalaureate Degree.

CAEL: Council for Adult and Experiential Learning.

CEEB: Former name of Advanced Placement (AP) exams.

Challenge Exams: Comprehensive examinations in a particular course of study. Given for the purpose of awarding credit in a specific course and/or waiving course prerequisites.

CLEP: College Level Examination Program.

Commencement: A ceremony where a class of graduates are assembled.

COPA: Council on Postsecondary Accreditation. All six regional accreditation bodies hold membership.

Credentials: Evidence of qualifications. A degree is an educational credential.

Credit: A measurement unit pertaining to coursework.

Credit Bank: a school that will evaluate learning experiences (coursework, exams, and others methods) and place them on an official transcript.

DANTES: Defense Activity for Non-Traditional Education Support.

Departmental Exams: See Challenge Exams.

Diploma: Written evidence of educational credentials, namely a degree.

Diploma Mill: A business or other concern issuing phony educational credentials. For more information, see Appendix C.

Electives: Areas of a degree requirement that students can meet with a wide array of courses.

Enrollment: Refers to registration for a course.

Experiential: Learning that occurs as a result of experiences outside the classroom. College-level experiences can be assessed for credit awards.

General Education: The portion of learning in a degree program that provides a broad range of knowledge.

GPA: Grade point average, a widely used measure of academic standing based on earned grade points.

Graduate: As a verb, the completion of a terminal degree and the graduation process. As an adjective it refers to postbaccalaureate study (master and doctorate).

GRE: Graduate Record Examination.

Independent Study: A course of study in which the student determines the content and/or pace of study, with minimum supervision by a teacher.

Individualized Degree Program: A degree where the student determines, with faculty and school staff, a customized course of study intended to lead to a degree.

Laboratory: The portion of a course that contains a hands-on element of learning.

Liberal Arts: Education outside the realm of hard science, generally comprising study in humanities, history, languages, and abstract sciences.

Lower Division: College-level study of an introductory nature.

Major: Primary concentrated study in a designated program area.

Master's Degree: A terminal degree program equivalent to two years of full-time study. A typical prerequisite for this degree is a baccalaureate degree.

Matriculate: To be admitted into a college with the intent of finishing a particular degree.

MBA: Master of Business Administration.

Minor: Secondary concentrated study in a designated area.

NATTS: National Association of Technical and Trade Schools.

NHSC: National Home Study Council.

PhD: Doctor of Philosophy, a type of doctorate degree.

Prerequisite: A course or series of courses that are required to be completed before enrolling in a more advanced course.

Prior Learning: See Experiential.

Quarter: A period of time delimiting a calendar for courses. Schools that use a quarter calendar can hold courses during four quarters of the year.

RCE: Regents College Exams, which are essentially the ACT PEP exams in the state of New York.

Registrar: A school's academic office or organization that records student enrollment and academic progress.

Semester: A period of time delimiting a calendar for courses. Schools that use a semester calendar can hold courses during two or three semesters of the year.

Transcript: A record of academic progress maintained by a school. Also refers to a financial aid transcript that records financial aid received.

Undergraduate: College-level study or standing prior to the fourth year.

Upper Division: College-level study of a nature that challenges those of junior and senior standing.

VCR: Video cassette recorder.

Colleges and Universities

Introduction

This digest of undergraduate and graduate alternative degree programs supplies information to help you decide which schools you'd like to request further information from. This should narrow down your list of potential schools. It will also keep you from having to go through a mailbag of promotional material.

Most of the information provided was developed with the participation and review of the schools listed. In addition to contact details, each school is outlined in five areas:

1. Degrees Offered
2. Credit-Earning Methods Offered/Accepted
3. Residency Required or External?
4. Cost Basis/Major Costs
5. Comments

Degrees Offered

This is a partial list of the degree options offered by the school. The degree level (associate, bachelor's, etc.) and, optionally, the major area of study are included. Some of the degrees are technical, others may have a different focus (for those on the management career ladder), and still others may have general, individualized, or independent study majors (or no major at all). The intent is to include all of the known technical degree programs as well as the more aggressive schools with flexible degree programs; in this way, the selection of nontraditional degree programs here covers people seeking specific technical degrees and technical professionals needing other accredited degrees.

Credit-Earning Methods Offered/Accepted

With this information you should be able to get a good idea about whether the school will permit you to use your preferred credit-earning method. Check carefully with each school you are interested in: Sometimes a school will offer a credit method for credit but will not accept a credit transfer of that same method (prior learning is a good example of this).

Residency Required or External?

Use this to get an idea of how many credits (if any) you'll need to earn while enrolled at each school and how often you'll have to visit the campus (if at all). If the degree can be earned externally, none of these restrictions exist.

Cost Basis/Major Costs

This is intended to give you an idea of what it takes to get going, as well as the ongoing tuition costs. Of course, you'll have other expenses (some significant), but if you're sensitive to price, this is a good indicator of costs.

Comments

This is miscellaneous information meant to give some depth to the school and its degree programs such as size, stability, and other details of how you can complete your degree.

■ ■ ■

Antioch University
School for Adult and Experiential Learning
800 Livermore Street
Yellow Springs, OH 45387
(513) 767-6325
Fax: (513) 767-1891

Degrees Offered: Individualized MA

Credit-Earning Methods Offered/Accepted: individualized study, transfer credit, independent study, prior learning/portfolio assessment

Residency Required or External? Required residency; maximum credit transfer of 15 credits (of approximately 50 total). Requires only two five-day seminars on campus.

Cost Basis/Major Costs:

- $400 enrollment fee
- $1,215 per quarter
- $50 per credit hour
- $300 prior learning evaluation

Comments: In this individualized master's program, you design a degree plan that interests you. Although it's an arts degree, many areas of study can be worked into this program. The student works with a faculty advisor and degree committee of the student's choice to plan and execute learning activities. The end result is a thesis that's presented on-campus. Average completion time is eight to ten quarters.

Accredited by: North Central Association of Colleges and Schools

■■■

Atlantic Union College

Adult Degree Program
P.O. Box 1000
South Lancaster, MA 01561
(508) 368-2300, (800) 282-2030 ext. 2300
Fax: (508) 368-2015

Degrees Offered: BA and BS in computer science and other majors

Credit-Earning Methods Offered/Accepted: individualized study, classroom study, transfer credit, independent study, college course exams, standardized exams, prior learning/portfolio assessment, employee training/company-sponsored education, military credit

Residency Required or External? Residency required; two six-month units of study with the minimum time on campus comprising one two-week seminar and one other short visit.

Cost Basis/Major Costs:

- $36 enrollment fee
- $2,986 per unit (six months)
- $150 per unit of evaluation

Comments: After using various methods to build up an initial transcript at Atlantic Union, the student can take advantage of six-month individualized study units, each equivalent to one semester of full-time study. Prior to each unit, the student attends a one-week seminar (given twice a year). Atlantic Union has graduated 400 people in 20 years, including a handful in its computer science program. The average cost to complete a degree is $6,000 to $9,000.

Accredited by: New England Association of Schools and Colleges, Inc.

■■■

Bradley University

Division of Continuing Education
118 Bradley Hall
Peoria, IL 61625
(309) 677-2523, (800) 552-1697

Degrees Offered: MS in electrical engineering, MS in mechanical engineering

Credit-Earning Methods Offered/Accepted: video and broadcast study, transfer credit

Residency Required or External? External; a maximum of six hours can be transferred for credit.

Cost Basis/Major Costs:

- $30 enrollment fee
- $246 to $307 per credit hour (part time)

Comments: This program is offered at remote sites in Illinois (at Moline, East Moline, Rock Island, and Davenport), where classroom instruction is given via video.

Accredited by: North Central Association of Colleges and Schools

■■■

Brigham Young University

Degrees by Independent Study
315 Harman Building
Provo, UT 84602
(801) 378-4351
Fax: (801) 378-3949

Degrees Offered: Bachelor of Independent Study

Credit-Earning Methods Offered/Accepted: transfer credit, independent study, standardized exams, individualized study

Residency Required or External? Residency required; 37 semester hours must be earned at BYU. On-campus attendance is required for a total of 11 weeks of seminars (five two-week and one one-week).

Cost Basis/Major Costs:

- $15 enrollment fee
- $7,000-plus for all tuition
- $200 fee for any standardized exam credit

Comments: This program features independent study in the liberal arts. It's very structured; there's little flexibility in course selections that are not technology-oriented. It takes from four to six years to complete.

Accredited by: The Northwest Association of Schools and Colleges

■■■

Burlington College

Independent Degree Program (IDP): Admissions
95 North Avenue
Burlington, VT 05401
(802) 862-9616

Degrees Offered: BA in individualized major

Credit-Earning Methods Offered/Accepted: individualized study, classroom study, transfer credit, independent study, standardized exams, prior learning/portfolio assessment, employee training/company-sponsored education, military credit, internships

Residency Required or External? Residency required; a minimum of 30 credits must be completed at Burlington. (You need 60 prior college credits to enroll, but some of these can be earned through exams and other evaluated methods.) Only required attendance is four-day residential weekend seminars in Burlington, Vermont, at the beginning of each semester.

Cost Basis/Major Costs:

- $3000 per semester

Comments: Students plan IDP semesters at each residential weekend seminar. Each semester gives the student the opportunity to earn up to 15 credits. The seminar fee is comprehensive, including room and board.

Accredited by: New England Association of Schools and Colleges, Inc.

■■■

Capital University

Adult Degree Program
Columbus, OH 43209
(614) 236-6996, (800) 289-6289

Degrees Offered: BA and BS in computer science, engineering, multidisciplinary studies, general studies; many nontechnical majors

Credit-Earning Methods Offered/Accepted: individualized study, classroom study, transfer credit, independent study, standardized exams, prior learning/portfolio assessment, employee training/company-sponsored education, military credit

Residency Required or External? Residency required; 30 out of the last 36 credit hours must be completed through Capital University.

Cost Basis/Major Costs:

- $225 per credit hour

Comments: The Adult Degree Program is not an off-campus program as such; attendance at one of Capital's three Ohio campuses (in Columbus, Cleveland, and Dayton) is required. To complete a degree, the student develops a learning contract and completes it according to agreed-upon methods (including any of the methods listed). Capital University reports that current enrollment is approximately 453. Due to the limited nature of evening lab courses, only a few students are pursuing technical degrees. (An option is to pursue these courses by using traditional study at another college.)

Accredited by: North Central Association of Colleges and Schools

■■■

Central Michigan University

Extended Degree Program
Rowe Hall 131
Mount Pleasant, MI 48859
(517) 774-7813, (800) 950-1144
Fax: (517) 774-3542

Degrees Offered: MS in software engineering administration, BS in industrial administration

Credit-Earning Methods Offered/Accepted: off-campus classroom study, transfer credit, independent study (accepts others and offers its own), tutorials, standardized exams, prior learning/portfolio assessment, employee training/company-sponsored education, planned experiences, military credit, learning packages

Residency Required or External? Residency required; in the 36-credit master's program, a maximum of 15 credits can be transferred—the rest must earned through Central Michigan. Of the 124

credits in the bachelor's program, a maximum of 94 may be transferred. The bachelor's program is only offered in Michigan.

Cost Basis/Major Costs:

- $40 enrollment fee
- $128/172 (extended bachelor's/master's) per credit hour

Comments: Central Michigan has off-campus learning sites at schools and military bases across the U.S. and Canada. Learning at these sites occurs in cohort groups of 20 to 30 students. If you can generate enough interest to form a cohort group of your own, Central Michigan can make arrangements to open a new site in your area. The school offers a relatively inexpensive graduate program.

Accredited by: North Central Association of Colleges and Schools

■■■

Charter Oak State College
Board for State Academic Awards
270 Farmington Avenue
Farmington, CT 06032-1934
(203) 677-0076

Degrees Offered: AA, AS, BA, and BS with the following technical concentrations: applied science and technology, computer science, and technology and management, as well as interdisciplinary studies, business, and other areas

Credit-Earning Methods Offered/Accepted: classroom study, transfer credit, independent study (accepts others and offers its own), college course exams, standardized exams, Charter Oak business proficiency tests, prior learning/portfolio assessment, employee training/company-sponsored education, certificates and licenses, military credit, special assessment of noncollegiate courses.

Residency Required or External? 100% external.

Cost Basis/Major Costs:

- $285/410 (in/out state) enrollment fee
- $195 program matriculation fee
- $200/315 (in/out state) annual advisement fee
- $150/225 (in/out state) portfolio review base fee
- $12 per portfolio credit attempted

Comments: Charter Oak has an excellent program. More than 3,000 people have graduated from Charter Oak—its wide range of credit-earning methods is one of the reasons. The school also awards moderate blocks of credit for passing various GRE subject exams. In many situations, this is a very inexpensive degree program.

Accredited by: New England Association of Schools and Colleges, Inc.

■■■

City University
14506 N.E. 20th, Suite D
Bellevue, WA 98007-3713
(206) 624-1688, (800) 422-4898
Fax: (206) 641-2017

Degrees Offered: BS in computer information systems, technology/engineering management, general studies, and telecommunications; various technology-oriented MBAs with concentration options in Asia/Pacific management, entrepreneurship, information systems, technology/engineering management, telecommunications management, and a master of education in education technology information systems

Credit-Earning Methods Offered/Accepted: classroom study, independent on-line study (Distance Learn), transfer credit, college course exams (accepts others and offers its own), standardized exams, prior learning/portfolio assessment, employee training/company-sponsored education, certificates and licenses, military credit, individualized study (directed study), placement exams

Residency Required or External? Can be 100% external. In the bachelor's program, a minimum of 45 credits must be earned through City University; in the master's program, up to 12 credits appropriate to the degree sought may be transferred.

Cost Basis/Major Costs:

- $152/210 (bachelor's/master's) per credit hour
- $50 enrollment fee

Comments: City University has a full menu of academic offerings including Distance Learn, many remote campuses on the west coast of the U.S. and Canada, intensive study, fast-track dual degrees, and a way for people without undergraduate degrees to be admitted to its MBA program (this requires either a Professional Engineer license or a Fundamentals of Engineering certificate). The main focus of City University is classroom-based degrees, but the wide range of options make it worth considering for the external student. City University isn't cheap, but it makes an ongoing effort to please its customers: Students may now evaluate learning options in Japan, as well as in a course of study related to total quality management (TQM).

Accredited by: The Northwest Association of Schools and Colleges

■■■

Colorado State University

SURGE: Division of Continuing Education
Spruce Hall
Fort Collins, CO 80523
(303) 491-5288, (800) 525-4950
Fax: (303) 491-7886

Degrees Offered: MS in chemical engineering, civil engineering, computer science, electrical engineering, interdisciplinary engineering, mechanical engineering

Credit-Earning Methods Offered/Accepted: video-based classroom study, transfer credit

Residency Required or External? 100% external.

Cost Basis/Major Costs:

- $250/350 (in/out state) per credit hour

Comments: Colorado SURGE has a very strong set of graduate degree programs with real academic standards. Students view video classes at existing SURGE sites (corporate or open) or by establishing their own SURGE site (which is easy according to the bulletin). SURGE is fully electronic, offering e-mail and fax communications with faculty and staff as well as video courses. SURGE is also affiliated with many consortiums and leading-edge corporate organizations.

Accredited by: North Central Association of Colleges and Schools

■■■

Columbia Union College

External Studies
7600 Flower Avenue
Takoma Park, MD 20912
(301) 270-9200, (800) 835-4212
Fax: (301) 270-1618

Degrees Offered: AA, AS, and BS in general studies

Credit-Earning Methods Offered/Accepted: independent study (mail), transfer credit, college course exams, standardized exams, prior learning/exam assessment, military credit

Residency Required or External? External; at least 30 credits must be earned through Columbia Union (may be done through independent study).

Cost Basis/Major Costs:

- $60 registration fee (per semester)
- $125 per credit hour

Comments: Coursework through Columbia Union may be done by independent study via the mail. No technical degrees are offered, but the general studies program may provide enough flexibility for technical professionals who could use any type of degree.

Accredited by: Middle States Association of Colleges and Schools

■■■

Eastern Oregon State College
External Degree Program
1410 L Avenue
La Grande, OR 97850-2899
(503) 962-3672, (800) 452-8639

Degrees Offered: Bachelor of Liberal Studies

Credit-Earning Methods Offered/Accepted: classroom study, transfer credit, independent study, standardized exams, prior learning/portfolio assessment, employee training/company-sponsored education, military credit, computer conferencing

Residency Required or External? Can be 100% external. A minimum of 45 credits must be earned under the supervision of Eastern faculty.

Cost Basis/Major Costs:

- $40 enrollment fee
- $200 initial advisement fee
- $50 annual advisement fee

Comments: Within Eastern Oregon's Bachelor of Liberal Studies degree program, it's possible to build a concentration option comprised of computer science. This is another program that, in the right situation, could be reasonably inexpensive to complete. Realistically, it requires proximity to face-to-face advising support at Eastern Oregon State College.

Accredited by: The Northwest Association of Schools and Colleges

■■■

Edison State College
101 West State
Trenton, NJ 08608-1176
(609) 984-1150
Fax: (609) 984-8447

Degrees Offered: AS in applied science and technology; BS in applied science and technology and business administration (data processing); other AS/BA programs tailored to technical studies. Many high-technology major areas of study are offered.

Credit-Earning Methods Offered/Accepted: transfer credit, guided independent study, college course exams, standardized exams, prior learning/portfolio assessment, employee training/company-sponsored education, certificates and licenses, military credit

Residency Required or External? External.

Cost Basis/Major Costs:

- $375/665 (NJ resident/nonresident) annual enrollment fee
- Approximately $5/10 (NJ resident/nonresident) per transfer credit hour (NJ residents)
- $10–15 per credit hour for portfolio evaluation

Comments: Many majors are offered in the engineering and technology areas, and many nontraditional ways of earning credit are provided. Those interested in an external degree would do well to check out Thomas Edison. Portfolio assessment is a favorite credit-building method, but this school also offers its own set of exams, guided study, video courses, computer-assisted services, and a credit bank. The school's excellent partnerships with companies in telecommunications, public utilities, and other technologies enable many to complete their degrees while they work. Thomas Edison is a standard among nontraditional schools and can be very inexpensive and fast.

Accredited by: Middle States Association of Colleges and Schools

■■■

Elizabethtown College
Center for Continuing Education
EXCEL Program
One Alpha Drive
Elizabethtown, PA 17022-2298
(717) 361-1141

Degrees Offered: Bachelor of Liberal Studies, Bachelor of Professional Studies

Credit-Earning Methods Offered/Accepted: classroom study, transfer credit, independent study, standardized exams, prior-learning assessment, military credit

Residency Required or External? Residency required; four all-day seminars must be completed.

Cost Basis/Major Costs:

- $2,580 program fee plus costs to earn credits

Comments: To be accepted to the EXCEL program, you must live within 400 miles of Elizabethtown College, have seven years of work experience in your major field, and have completed a minimum of 50 semester hours of college study. While the degrees are not technology-oriented, they may work for those less concerned with that aspect.

Accredited by: Middle States Association of Colleges and Schools

■■■

Embry-Riddle Aeronautical University
Independent Studies
600 South Clyde Morris Boulevard
Daytona, FL 32114
(904) 239-6390, (800) 222-ERAU
Fax: (904) 239-6927

Degrees Offered: AS, BS, and MS in electrical engineering, computer science, professional aeronautics, aerospace engineering, avionics computer engineering, and many others

Credit-Earning Methods Offered/Accepted: classroom study, transfer credit, independent study, standardized tests, course examinations, employee training/company-sponsored education, certificates and licenses (FAA), military credit

Residency Required or External? Can be 100% external.

Cost Basis/Major Costs:

- $135 per credit hour (undergraduate through continuing education)
- $191 per credit hour (graduate through continuing education)

Comments: Embry-Riddle has, in addition to its main campus, resident centers at more than 60 sites across the U.S. and Europe. It also has a department of independent studies through which you can obtain a degree that requires no attendance at an Embry-

Riddle campus or resident center (not all degrees are offered in every program, however). Courses and degrees are related to aviation and aerospace.

Accredited by: Southern Association of Colleges and Schools

∎∎∎

Empire State College
State University of New York
Center for Distance Learning
2 Union Avenue
Saratoga Springs, NY 12866-4309
(518) 587-2100

Degrees Offered: BA in interdisciplinary studies and other major areas

Credit-Earning Methods Offered/Accepted: independent study, classroom study, transfer credit, college course exams, standardized exams, employee training/company-sponsored education, military credit

Residency Required or External? Can be 100% external.

Cost Basis/Major Costs:

- $200 matriculation fee
- $90/107 (matriculated/nonmatriculated) per credit hour

Comments: The Center for Distance Learning at Empire State College requires no classroom attendance. Independent study course materials include textbooks, course guides, and video/audio tapes. Contact is maintained with faculty through the phone, mail, or computer. Each student's degree program is designed in response to his or her learning interests, goals, and needs.

Accredited by: Middle States Association of Colleges and Schools

∎∎∎

Evergreen State College
Olympia, WA 98505
(206) 866-6000
Fax: (206) 866-6823

Degrees Offered: BS in computer studies

Credit-Earning Methods Offered/Accepted: seminars, core studies, prior learning/portfolio assessment, individualized study

Residency Required or External? Residency required.

Cost Basis/Major Costs:

- $1,785/6,297 (WA resident/nonresident) nine-month tuition

Comments: Evergreen is nontraditional in the sense of educational approach, not in credit-earning methods. This school offers year-long study programs entitled Data to Information, Computability and Cognition, Student-Originated Software, and Science of the Mind. Evergreen definitely offers something different—learning that looks like fun.

Accredited by: The Northwest Association of Schools and Colleges

■■■

Indiana Institute of Technology
Extended Studies Division
1600 East Washington Boulevard
Fort Wayne, IN 46803
(219) 422-5561, (800) 288-1766

Degrees Offered: AS and BS in business administration, BS in human services management

Credit-Earning Methods Offered/Accepted: transfer credit, independent study, standardized exams, prior learning/portfolio assessment, military credit

Residency Required or External? 100% external; a minimum of 30 credits must be earned through Indiana Tech (15 credits minimum for an associate's degree).

Cost Basis/Major Costs:

- $50 enrollment fee
- $153 per credit hour
- $20 per credit through portfolio assessment

Comments: No technical degree programs are offered, but a degree carrying the Indiana Tech stamp may prove useful to some, especially those considering a move from engineering to marketing. Indiana Tech builds this program on its own correspondence study courses, which may be used to complete an entire degree. If you live near Fort Wayne or Indianapolis, you might be interested in the accelerated degree program. Interestingly, this school requires all students to pass competency tests before graduation.

Accredited by: North Central Association of Colleges and Schools

···

Indiana University

Systemwide General Studies
Owen Hall 101
Bloomington, IN 47405
(812) 855-3693, (800) 334-1011
Fax: (812) 855-8680

Degrees Offered: Associate of General Studies, Bachelor of General Studies

Credit-Earning Methods Offered/Accepted: classroom study, transfer credit, independent study (accepts others and has its own large program), college course exams (some restrictions), standardized exams, prior learning/portfolio assessment, military credit

Residency Required or External? Can be 100% external; requires that at least 25% of the degree be earned from Indiana University (this can generally be completed through independent study courses).

Cost Basis/Major Costs:

- $25 admission fee
- $74 per credit hour

Comments: For those inclined to independent study, this can be a reasonably inexpensive to moderately priced degree. Computer science is a recognized subject field toward which you could lean this degree program. The Indiana University independent study program is one of the largest in the country, with 18,000 students currently enrolled.

Accredited by: North Central Association of Colleges and Schools

···

Johnson State College

External Degree Program
Johnson, VT 05656
(802) 635-2356

Degrees Offered: BA, BS

Credit-Earning Methods Offered/Accepted: classroom study (and weekend classes), transfer credit, independent study, standardized exams, military credit

Residency Required or External? Residency required; monthly workshops and a minimum of 30 credits must be taken through Johnson State College.

Cost Basis/Major Costs:

- $40 enrollment fee
- $115 per credit hour

Comments: Only Vermont residents may be admitted to this program, which is basically a general studies degree within the BA and BS frameworks. While there are no specific technology degree programs, an area of concentration might be built into the BS program.

Accredited by: New England Association of Schools and Colleges, Inc.

■■■

Mary Baldwin College
Adult Degree Program
Staunton, VA 24401
(703) 887-7703, (800) 822-2460

Degrees Offered: BA in computer science/business administration, mathematics/computer science; other liberal arts majors

Credit-Earning Methods Offered/Accepted: classroom study, transfer credit, independent study, college course exams, standardized exams, prior learning/portfolio assessment, employee training/company-sponsored education, certificates and licenses, military credit

Residency Required or External? External; requires a visit to campus for an orientation session. There are three regional offices in Virginia.

Cost Basis/Major Costs:

- $25 enrollment fee, plus costs to earn credits
- $245 per credit hour (if taken from Mary Baldwin College)
- $200 portfolio evaluation

Comments: Once you've completed orientation, you can work with a Mary Baldwin tutor or an approved off-campus tutor in your own area. You must complete a minimum of 33 credits through Mary Baldwin College, but you aren't required to take on-campus courses at Mary Baldwin. This has the potential to be a very quick and inexpensive degree. The Adult Degree Program is a stable program with over 700 students currently enrolled.

Accredited by: Southern Association of Colleges and Schools

■■■

Mind Extension University

9697 East Mineral Avenue
Englewood, CO 80112-9920
(800) 777-6463

Degrees Offered: MBA, MA, and BA degree completion

Credit-Earning Methods Offered/Accepted: studying via cable TV plus other accepted methods of transfer and evaluation

Residency Required or External? External.

Cost Basis/Major Costs:

- $148 per undergraduate credit hour (average)
- $300 per graduate credit hour

Comments: Mind Extension University is a cable TV channel that delivers video courses to various universities, including a consortium of nine well-known schools. At this school, you matriculate into a degree program, tape your courses (you must make sure your local cable TV supplier carries the MEU channel or satellite reception, otherwise you'll have to pay extra to get tapes mailed to you), and then work through the taped lectures and coursework on your own time. It's a concept that seems to work well. No technology degrees are offered yet, but this school is an interesting alternative.

Accredited by: All consortium schools have regional accreditation.

■■■

National Technological University

700 Centre Avenue
Fort Collins, CO 80526
(303) 484-6050
Fax: (303) 484-0668

Degrees Offered: MS in electrical engineering, computer science, computer engineering, engineering management, health physics, hazardous waste management, manufacturing systems engineering, material science engineering, software engineering, management of technology, and special majors (mechanical)

Credit-Earning Methods Offered/Accepted: mostly the school's own satellite courses, some transfer credit

Residency Required or External? External.

Cost Basis/Major Costs:

- $445 per credit hour

Comments: National Technological University provides classes via satellite to 430 corporate and college locations across the country. To attend, you must either have access at your work site now, or convince your company to install the equipment and make the necessary arrangements. The school brings the top faculty of 45 engineering universities to these sites and has issued 255 MS degrees since 1986. An MS degree can be earned in two to three years.

Accredited by: North Central Association of Colleges and Schools

■■■

New York Institute of Technology
American Open University
211 Carlton Avenue
Central Islip, NY 11722
(516) 686-7712, (800) 222-NYIT
Fax: (516) 348-0912

Degrees Offered: BS in general studies and bachelor of professional studies in general studies

Credit-Earning Methods Offered/Accepted: on-line classroom study, transfer credit, independent study, college course exams, standardized exams, prior learning/portfolio assessment, employee training/company-sponsored education, military credit

Residency Required or External? Can be 100% external; a minimum of 30 credits must be earned through the university.

Cost Basis/Major Costs:

- $3,645 per semester (if full time)
- $243 per credit hour (if part time)
- $11 per hour of on-line time

Comments: This is an on-line school where you use your PC or Macintosh to put you into the electronic classroom via phone. The BS degrees encompass interdisciplinary study and can be tailored, to an extent, to suit the student. On-line courses work like independent study, with the exception of the professor's electronic conferences, which simulate the classroom environment.

Accredited by: Middle States Association of Colleges and Schools

■■■

Northwood Institute
3225 Cook Road
Midland, MI 48640-2398
(517) 837-4411

Degrees Offered: associate's and bachelor's degrees in business with dual majors in computer science/management and computer information/management

Credit-Earning Methods Offered/Accepted: classroom study (weekend and evening), transfer credit, independent study, college course exams, standardized exams, prior learning/portfolio assessment, military credit, individualized study

Residency Required or External? Residency required; all but approximately 12 credit hours (out of 180) can be completed off-campus.

Cost Basis/Major Costs:

- $15 enrollment fee
- $175 per quarter credit hour (campus courses)
- $45 per quarter credit hour (independent study)
- $600 evaluation fee

Comments: Northwood Institute offers an external plan of study supported through on-campus seminars, along with remote extension locations (10 sites in the U.S.). The portfolio-assessment program is generous to those with lots of experience; it permits 144 of 180 quarter credits (for a bachelor's degree) to be earned with this method. Other innovative methods available include take-home and open-book exams, work projects, and mini-courses. This is a relatively large external program, with more than 5,000 students.

Accredited by: North Central Association of Colleges and Schools

■■■

Nova University
Center for Computer and Information Sciences
3301 College Avenue
Fort Lauderdale, FL 33314
(305) 475-7085, (800) 541-6682 ext. 7085

Degrees Offered: Doctor of Education in computer education, Doctor of Science, and Master of Science

Credit-Earning Methods Offered/Accepted: classroom study, transfer credit

Residency-Required or External? Residency required; requires classroom attendance, but classes may be held at any site where there is sufficient interest.

Cost Basis/Major Costs:

- $6,000 per year

Comments: Field-based study has been highly developed over the years by the innovative Nova University. It makes use of regional- or site-based study where a professor can be sent for classroom sessions. The school also emphasizes on-line communications for these education-oriented degrees. The more complex nature of course delivery and the degree program warrants careful investigation. The field-based study program has an enrollment of 6,000 students across the U. S., mostly clustered in Florida, Arizona, and Nevada.

Accredited by: Southern Association of Colleges and Schools

■ ■ ■

Ohio University
External Student Program
302 Tupper Hall
Athens, OH 45701
(614) 593-2150, (800) 444-2910
Fax: (614) 593-2901

Degrees Offered: AS, AA, and Bachelor of Specialized Studies; other associate degrees

Credit-Earning Methods Offered/Accepted: classroom study, transfer credit, independent study, college course exams, standardized exams, prior learning/portfolio assessment, employee training/company-sponsored education, certificates and licenses, military credit, individualized study

Residency Required or External? Can be 100% external.

Cost Basis/Major Costs:

- $60 annual fee plus other costs to earn credits
- $48 per quarter hour for correspondence independent study
- $26 per quarter hour for course credit by examination

Comments: This is a good school with a long history of helping students complete their degrees off-campus. Ohio University is known for its correspondence courses and course examinations; these offerings may be used to meet many of the general education requirements for these degrees (including course exams in the engineering and technology areas). The Bachelor of Specialized Studies is particularly apt for those who can't make it to the campus but want to design their own career-oriented degrees.

Accredited by: North Central Association of Colleges and Schools

...

Oklahoma City University
Competency-Based Degrees
2501 North Blackwelder
Oklahoma City, OK 73106
(405) 521-5265

Degrees Offered: bachelor's degrees

Credit-Earning Methods Offered/Accepted: Oklahoma City University used to accept classroom study, transfer credit, independent study, standardized exams, prior learning/portfolio assessment, directed readings, employee training/company-sponsored education, and military credit.

Residency Required or External? Residency required.

Comments: This program has apparently changed from a mostly external program to something else (largely unknown despite intensive efforts to find out). It appears, however, that external degrees have been eliminated. If you live near Oklahoma City, it may be worth a phone call to find out for sure.

Accredited by: North Central Association of Colleges and Schools

...

Pace University
One Martine Avenue
White Plains, NY 10606
(914) 422-4191

Degrees Offered: BS in professional computer studies

Credit-Earning Methods Offered/Accepted: classroom study, transfer credit, standardized exams, prior learning (Life Experience Learning), military credit, course-challenge exams

Residency Required or External? Residency required.

Cost Basis/Major Costs:

- $310 enrollment fee

Comments: This traditional school realizes that many people are working in the computer industry without degrees. It offers plenty of classes but specifically supports Life Experience Learning for credit at all three campuses in the New York City area. Pace University requires that students take an ICCP exam.

Accredited by: Middle States Association of Colleges and Schools

■■■

Pennsylvania State University
Extended Letters, Arts, Sciences Degree
Department of Independent Learning
128 Mitchell Building
University Park, PA 16802-3693
(814) 865-5403, (800) 458-3617
Fax: (814) 865-3290

Degrees Offered: associate's degree in liberal arts or business administration

Credit-Earning Methods Offered/Accepted: transfer credit, independent study, certain CLEP exams

Residency Required or External? External.

Cost Basis/Major Costs:

- $90 per credit hour

Comments: If you need an associate's degree, you can earn 57 of the 60 necessary credits directly from Penn State. No higher external degree is available from this school, but the array of more than 200 independent study and video courses, some in technology, computer and engineering areas, is worth a look.

Accredited by: Middle States Association of Colleges and Schools

■■■

Prescott College
Adult Degree Program
220 Grove Avenue
Prescott, AZ 86301
(602) 776-7116

Degrees Offered: BA in management and individualized liberal arts; other areas

Credit-Earning Methods Offered/Accepted: independent (mentored) study, study contracts, portfolio assessment, individualized study

Residency Required or External? Mostly external; the only required visits are two three-day sessions.

Cost Basis/Major Costs:

- $2,700 per six months of enrollment

Comments: This isn't a technology school, but it may be useful to students who want a degree and don't mind a BA. The individualized program can be leaned toward your specific interests.

Accredited by: North Central Association of Colleges and Schools

■■■

Regis University
RECEP
3333 Regis Boulevard
Denver, CO 80221
(303) 458-3530
Fax: (303) 458-4273

Degrees Offered: BS in computer information systems; other areas

Credit-Earning Methods Offered/Accepted: classroom study, transfer credit, college course exams, standardized exams, prior learning/portfolio assessment, employee training/company-sponsored education, military credit

Residency Required or External? Residency required; 30 required semester hours required plus lots of on-campus attendance.

Cost Basis/Major Costs:

- $60 enrollment fee
- $176 per credit hour
- $45 per credit of challenge exams

Comments: Regis University is more of a traditional school with an array of credit-building options. It has five sites in the Denver area, each providing instruction and full academic services. Courses are in an accelerated, interactive format.

Accredited by: North Central Association of Colleges and Schools

■■■

Roger Williams College
Open Program
One Old Ferry Road
Bristol, RI 02809
(401) 254-3530
Fax: (401) 254-3480

Degrees Offered: BA and BS in many areas including computer information systems, computer science, engineering (civil, electrical, or mechanical), industrial technology

Credit-Earning Methods Offered/Accepted: classroom study, transfer credit, independent study, college course exams, standardized exams, prior learning/portfolio assessment, employee training/company-sponsored education, military credit

Residency Required or External? May be 100% external; some short visits are usually necessary. Thirty credits minimum are required while the student is enrolled at Roger Williams.

Cost Basis/Major Costs:

- $365 per credit hour (minimum 24 hours at this rate)

Comments: This is a solid program that delivers technology degrees with nontraditional flexibility and speed. While the minimum of 30 credits is a lot, the overall cost can be moderate if other credits are already earned.

Accredited by: New England Association of Schools and Colleges, Inc.

■■■

St. Edwards University
New College
3001 South Congress
Austin, TX 78704
(512) 448-8717
Fax: (512) 448-8492

Degrees Offered: bachelor's degree in many majors

Credit-Earning Methods Offered/Accepted: classroom study, transfer credit, independent study, college course exams, standardized exams, portfolio assessment, employee training/company-sponsored education, military credit, individualized study

Residency Required or External? Residency required; minimum of four on-campus courses.

Cost Basis/Major Costs:

- $25 enrollment fee
- $276 per credit hour
- $60 portfolio evaluation/tuition fees per credit hour

Comments: This isn't a correspondence school because it tends toward on-campus learning methods, but it does support off-campus methods as well.

Accredited by: Southern Association of Colleges and Schools

■ ■ ■

Skidmore College
University Without Walls
Saratoga Springs, NY 12866
(518) 584-5000

Degrees Offered: BA and BS, but not in technical fields

Credit-Earning Methods Offered/Accepted: classroom study, transfer credit, independent study, college course exams, standardized exams, prior learning/portfolio assessment, employee training/company-sponsored education, military credit, individualized study

Residency Required or External? Mostly external; requires three short visits.

Cost Basis/Major Costs:

- $1,600 annual enrollment fee plus other costs to complete degree

Comments: Skidmore is not of interest to those with hard requirements for technical degrees. It's included here in case you can get by with a business or liberal arts degree.

Accredited by: Middle States Association of Colleges and Schools

■ ■ ■

Stephens Colleges
College Without Walls
Campus Box 2083
Columbia, MO 65215
(314) 876-7125, (800) 388-7579

Degrees Offered: associate's and bachelor's degrees in student-initiated majors

Credit-Earning Methods Offered/Accepted: classroom study, transfer credit, independent study, standardized exams, prior learning/portfolio assessment, employee training/company-sponsored education, military credit, individualized study, short-format courses

Residency Required or External? Mostly external; attendance is required at either a week or double weekend seminar.

Cost Basis/Major Costs:

- $50 enrollment fee
- $210 per credit hour (equivalent payable in larger amounts)
- $625 prior learning evaluation

Comments: This school is option for students who desire a primarily off-campus degree and are willing to accept a nontechnology degree (or to create their own). Students are assigned an advisor who helps them plan a program of study and assists them until graduation.

Accredited by: North Central Association of Colleges and Schools

■■■

Syracuse University
Independent Study Degree Programs
610 East Fayette Street
Syracuse, NY 13244-6020
(315) 443-3284
Fax: (315) 443-1928

Degrees Offered: BA in liberal studies, MBA

Credit-Earning Methods Offered/Accepted: classroom study, transfer credit, independent study, college course exams, standardized exams, prior learning/portfolio assessment, employee training/company-sponsored education. Certificates/licenses and military credit are also considered.

Residency Required or External? Residency required; regular visits to Syracuse campus are mandatory.

Cost Basis/Major Costs:

- $40 application fee
- $262/432 (undergraduate/graduate) per credit hour

Comments: This is an independent study-based degree program of interest to those who could use the BA degree and could handle the regular campus visits (about one day per course must be taken through Syracuse University).

Accredited by: Middle States Association of Colleges and Schools

■■■

Trinity College
Individualized Degree Program (IDP)
Hartford, CT 06106-3100
(203) 297-2150

Degrees Offered: bachelor's degree with majors in computer science, engineering, and others

Credit-Earning Methods Offered/Accepted: classroom study, independent study units, standardized exams

Residency Required or External? Mostly external in some fields (with frequent communication with faculty). Sixteen hours must be completed at Trinity.

Cost Basis/Major Costs:

- $7,200 per credit year (approximate)

Comments: If you're interested in designing your own individualized degree program, this is a worthwhile option, especially if you live in Connecticut or can make arrangements to visit the campus periodically. Well-regarded in New England, Trinity is a private school with an enrollment of less than 2,000.

Accredited by: New England Association of Schools and Colleges, Inc.

■■■

Troy State University
External Degree Program
P.O. Box 4419
Montgomery, AL 36103-4419
(205) 834-1400

Degrees Offered: AS in general education, BS and BA in professional studies

Credit-Earning Methods Offered/Accepted: classroom study, transfer credit, independent study, college course exams, learning contracts, standardized exams, prior learning assessment, employee training/company-sponsored education, military credit

Residency Required or External? External; one orientation session required that can be waived if you live more than 200 miles away.

Cost Basis/Major Costs:

- $50 enrollment fee
- $46/66 (Alabama resident/nonresident) per quarter credit hour
- $100 annual participation fee (after first year)

Comments: No degrees directly applicable to technology are offered, but Troy State provides solid general education that can help some people who simply need any degree. Moderately priced (even for out-of-state students), Troy State offers a good selection of independent study contract courses that can help you accomplish most degree requirements.

Accredited by: Southern Association of Colleges and Schools

■■■

Union Institute
440 East McMillan Street
Cincinnati, OH 45206-1947
(513) 861-6400, (800) 543-0366

Degrees Offered: BS, BA, PhD

Credit-Earning Methods Offered/Accepted: classroom study, transfer credit, independent study, college course exams, standardized exams, prior learning/portfolio assessment, employee training/company-sponsored education, military credit, individualized study

Residency Required or External? Mostly external; the undergraduate Distant Learner Program requires one weekend orientation visit to one of the school's five campuses. A minimum of 35 days (orientation, peer days, and seminars) must be completed on campus by graduate students.

Cost Basis/Major Costs:

- $2,175 per quarter (undergraduate)
- $2,484 per quarter (graduate)

Comments: With five locations (Los Angeles, Miami, San Diego, Cincinnati, and Sacramento), Union Institute may be a valid commute option for many individuals; with the Distant Learner Program, it's even more accessible, though more expensive than other alternatives. Union Institute uses a four-quarter-per-year schedule with no breaks so students can complete their degrees at an accelerated rate. Current enrollment is approximately 1,000 (doctorate) and 400 (undergraduate). No direct technical degrees are offered, but this program may be of interest to those who feel capable of putting together an individualized program.

Accredited by: North Central Association of Colleges and Schools

■■■

University of Alabama
New College External Degree Program (EXD)
P.O. Box 870182
Tuscaloosa, AL 35486-0182
(205) 348-6000
Fax: (205) 348-7022

Degrees Offered: BS in applied sciences; other BA and BS degrees

Credit-Earning Methods Offered/Accepted: classroom study, transfer credit, independent study, standardized exams, prior learning/portfolio assessment, employee training/company-sponsored education, military credit, individualized study project (contract learning)

Residency Required or External? Mostly external; attendance at a two-and-a-half-day seminar in Tuscaloosa, Alabama, is required (two hours of credit are awarded).

Cost Basis/Major Costs:

- $75 annual participation fee
- $400 seminar fee
- $83 per credit hour

Comments: You must look closely at this program to see if the degree will work for you; at this writing, there is an 18- to 24-month waiting period for the required planning seminar. Students are advised of credit options while they wait. Otherwise, the EXD program is reasonably flexible in design, is modestly priced (in many circumstances), and has been around since 1973. A minimum of 32 hours of credit must be completed under the guidance of the EXD program.

Accredited by: Southern Association of Colleges and Schools

■■■

University of Evansville
Center for Continuing Education
External Studies Program
1800 Lincoln Avenue
Evansville, IN 47722
(812) 479-2981

Degrees Offered: external BA and BS in individualized majors

Credit-Earning Methods Offered/Accepted: classroom study, transfer credit, independent study, college course exams, standardized exams, prior learning/portfolio assessment, employee training/company-sponsored education, certificates and licenses, military credit, individualized study

Residency Required or External? Residency required; 24 hours of credits must be earned from the University of Evansville and a two-day on-campus planning workshop is required.

Cost Basis/Major Costs:

- $130 enrollment/advising fee
- $25 per credit hour of experiential or challenge exams
- $170 per credit hour for evening courses
- $310 per credit hour for day courses

Comments: The external BA/BS is for people in Evansville or who can get to Evansville for the 24 credit hours of coursework. No technical- or science-oriented degrees are offered, but this school has a good selection of credit-earning options that are worth considering for those in the area. It's a small program with a yearly average of 30 enrollees.

Accredited by: North Central Association of Colleges and Schools

■■■

University of Idaho
College of Engineering
Video Outreach
Janssen Engineering
Moscow, ID 83843
(208) 885-6373, (800) 824-2889
Fax: (208) 885-6165

Degrees Offered: MS and ME in civil engineering, computer engineering, computer science, electrical engineering, geological engineering, psychology/human factors, and mechanical engineering

Credit-Earning Methods Offered/Accepted: video courses, transfer credit

Residency Required or External? External.

Cost Basis/Major Costs:

- $275 per credit hour (graduate)

Comments: This external master's degree program covers many engineering areas entirely by videotape. University of Idaho has put together a well-constructed degree program that offers both thesis and nonthesis versions. This means you may complete the degree with only courses if you want or need to. The price is reasonable (relative to some of the other graduate options), and a four-year schedule of video class offerings is published, with a complete bulletin mailed every term. If you are undecided about matriculating into the program or are interested in the video courses for another purpose, you can take specific course only, as well. (This is true of some undergraduate offerings also.) This engineering program has 400 students presently enrolled and graduates 50 to 60 every year (60% live out of Idaho).

Accredited by: Northwest Association of Schools and Colleges

■■■

University of Maryland

University College: Open Learning
University Boulevard at Adelphi Road
College Park, MD 20742-1660
(301) 985-7000
Fax: (301) 454-0399

Degrees Offered: bachelor's degree in technology management

Credit-Earning Methods Offered/Accepted: classroom study, transfer credit, independent study, telephone conferencing, college course exams, standardized exams, prior learning/portfolio assessment, employee training/company-sponsored education, certificates and licenses, military credit, individualized study, seminars, co-op

Residency Required or External? Can be external.

Cost Basis/Major Costs:

- $30 enrollment fee
- $145 per semester credit hour
- $155 per semester credit hour

Comments: The Open Learning courses are offered in three- and six-credit options which offers more intense courses for students. This college has been in business for 40 years and in any given year serves more than 90,000 adults in more than 20 countries. Probably the most striking aspect of this program is the degree concentration itself; it's one of the few for those on the management ladder who seek a bachelor's degree. It's worth a look even if you aren't located in the area.

Accredited by: Middle States Association of Colleges and Schools

■■■

University of Massachusetts

College of Engineering
Video Instructional Program
113 Marcus Hall
Amherst, MA 01003
(413) 545-0063
Fax: (413) 545-1227
E-mail: vip@ecs.umass.edu

Degrees Offered: MS in electrical and computer engineering; MS in engineering management

Credit-Earning Methods Offered/Accepted: videotape instruction, satellite instruction, short courses, transfer credit

Residency Required or External? Can be completed externally.

Cost Basis/Major Costs:

- $1,000 per course tuition (11 or 12 courses to complete)

Comments: This is a mature video-based delivery system that leads to the listed graduate degrees. Since 1990, the school has graduated 75 students, and the annual number of graduates has increased steadily. Since the UMass video program has been active for a long time, video instruction quality is better than average; in fact, what you view is UMass faculty teaching actual courses to students. The program is not like a correspondence school—you must get on the semester track and stick with it (there are extension requests, though). Courses may be brought to places of employment by satellite, or you may choose to have videotapes sent to your home; in both cases, assignments are mailed in. The College of Engineering has ABET accreditation.

Accredited by: New England Association of Schools and Colleges, Inc.

■■■

University of Massachusetts
Montague House
University Without Walls
Amherst, MA 01003
(413) 545-1378

Degrees Offered: BA and BS in individualized degrees

Credit-Earning Methods Offered/Accepted: classroom study, transfer credit, independent study, college course exams, standardized exams, prior learning/portfolio assessment, military credit, individualized study, internship

Residency Required or External? Mostly external; visits to campus are required for some coursework as well as for planning, evaluation, and supervision.

Cost Basis/Major Costs:

- $90 per credit hour (standard resident fees)

Comments: Since 1971, the University Without Walls program at the University of Massachusetts (UMass) has graduated more than 1,500 people who designed their own degree programs (with the help of advisors and faculty). The program cannot be completed through correspondence; while most students complete much of their work at the Amherst or Springfield campuses, those willing to locate faculty and other help can use independent study and other methods of learning to complete considerable coursework. This is a good program that has served many in the Massachusetts high-tech workforce.

Accredited by: New England Association of Schools and Colleges, Inc.

■■■

University of Minnesota
University College
Program for Individualized Learning
107 Armory
15 Church Street SE
Minneapolis, MN 55455
(612) 624-4020

Degrees Offered: BA and BS with areas of concentration

Credit-Earning Methods Offered/Accepted: directed individualized study, classroom study, transfer credit, independent study, college course exams, standardized exams, prior learning/portfolio assessment, employee training/company-sponsored education, certificates and licenses, military credit

Residency Required or External? Residency required; regular visits to the campus required during the year for (at least) advising and seminars.

Cost Basis/Major Costs:

- $852 per stage plus other costs for courses
- $50 continuing registration

Comments: The Program for Individualized Learning serves independent students who wish to design and complete a program of study that incorporates a variety of learning resources. This program is primarily available to those residing in Minnesota. The program itself uses four stages: admissions, degree planning, program implementation, and graduation. Contact with advisors is a crucial part of this program. Approximately 500 students are enrolled in programs offered by University College.

Accredited by: North Central Association of Colleges and Schools

■■■

University of Oklahoma

College of Liberal Studies
1700 Asp Avenue
Norman, OK 73037
(405) 325-1061, (800) 522-4389

Degrees Offered: Bachelor of Liberal Studies, Master of Liberal Studies

Credit-Earning Methods Offered/Accepted: classroom study, transfer credit, independent study, college course exams, standardized exams, employee training/company-sponsored education, military credit, individualized study

Residency Required or External? Mostly external; attendance at three to five seminars is required (25 to 45 days total; seminars are 5 to 10 days each).

Cost Basis/Major Costs:

- $3,168/10,609 (resident/nonresident) for bachelor's degree if you have an associate's degree or equivalent
- $2,040/6,464 (resident/nonresident) for master's degree

Comments: Established more than 30 years ago as one of the first nontraditional degree programs for adults, this liberal studies program maintains its interdisciplinary goals and service features. Adjectives that characterize these degrees are flexible, self-paced, and inexpensive (even for nonresidents of Oklahoma). Seminars are given on the University of Oklahoma campus in order to introduce and direct each phase of study. (At the end of the degree program a seminar is held to present results). A good portion of the students are not Oklahoma residents, so the program seems to be working for out-of-staters. These are individualized study programs where you design your degree with the help of advisors and faculty and then complete the requirements. It's a good program and worth checking out if the degree will work for you and you can manage the travel to Oklahoma.

Accredited by: North Central Association of Colleges and Schools

■■■

University of South Florida

SUS BIS Program
4202 East Fowler
Tampa, FL 33260-8400
(813) 974-4058

Degrees Offered: Bachelor of Independent Studies

Credit-Earning Methods Offered/Accepted: classroom study, transfer credit, guided independent study, comprehensive exams, standardized exams, prior learning, accelerated tutorial or reading program

Residency Required or External? Mostly external; attendance at a single two-week seminar is required.

Cost Basis/Major Costs:

- $55/214 (resident/nonresident) per credit hour

Comments: This is a pretty generic degree with lots of room for customization within the constraints of the usual general education degree. It's offered at a modest price for Florida residents and is a smaller program with approximately 150 graduates since 1972.

Accredited by: Southern Association of Colleges and Schools

■■■

The University of the State of New York
Regents College
1450 Western Avenue
Albany, NY 12203-3524
(518) 474-3703

Degrees Offered: AS and BS in technology, AS and BS in electronics technology, BS in computer technology, AS in computer software, BS in computer information systems, AS in nuclear technology, BS in nuclear technology

Credit-Earning Methods Offered/Accepted: transfer credit, independent study, college course exams, standardized exams, specialized assessment, employee training/company-sponsored education, certificates and licenses, military credit

Residency Required/External? 100% external.

Cost Basis/Major Costs:

- $480 enrollment fee (covers first year)
- $240 annual fee

Comments: With more than 55,000 graduates, Regents College is one of the two most successful nontraditional colleges in the U.S. (Thomas Edison State College is the other). Regents offers no courses of its own; in fact, it has no campus. Degrees can be inexpensive and quick because Regents accepts the use of the GRE subject exams. The University of the State of New York is the oldest state-governed school system in the country. Although it doesn't offer portfolio assessment, it does offer special assessment. If you're looking for a degree without a large math requirement, check into the two technology degrees. Nearly everyone considering nontraditional schools should explore Regents. Regents also has a credit bank option.

Accredited by: Middle States Association of Colleges and Schools

■ ■ ■

University of Wisconsin-Madison
Engineering Professional Development
432 North Lake Street
Madison, WI 53706
(608) 263-2055, (800) 442-6460
Fax: (608) 262-4096

Degrees Offered: Professional Development (PD) in engineering

Credit-Earning Methods Offered/Accepted: classroom study, independent study, transfer courses, seminars, short courses, workshops, video/satellite courses, continuing education units (CEUs), and professional registration

Residency Required or External? Can be external.

Cost Basis/Major Costs:
- $20 enrollment fee
- $600 independent study project
- $700–800 per course

Comments: The PD isn't a master's degree, but 20% of the people taking this study course already have a graduate degree (a bachelor's degree is required for admittance). This course of study, which can take up to seven years, seems to work well for people who integrate their study with career goals, particularly in professional engineering fields. If you're interested in a PD and a nontraditional approach, contact this school. The materials it sends are very good at explaining the program and the value of a PD in general.

Accredited by: The school is accredited by the North Central Association of Colleges and Schools. The PD degree program is not accredited by agencies such as ABET, which does not accredit any graduate programs.

■ ■ ■

Upper Iowa University
External Degree Program
Box 1861
Fayette, IA 52142
(319) 425-5252, (800) 533-4150
Fax: (319) 425-5310

Degrees Offered: BS (business/management-oriented)

Credit-Earning Methods Offered/Accepted: classroom study, transfer credit, independent study, standardized exams, prior learning/portfolio assessment, company-sponsored education, certificates and licenses, military credit, individualized study, summer session (IEXL)

Residency Required or External? External.

Cost Basis/Major Costs:

- $25 enrollment fee
- $120 per credit hour
- $50 portfolio evaluation fee per credit hour

Comments: No technical degrees are offered, but this program is useful for those heading up the management track. Independent study courses are available to meet degree requirements. You must complete a minimum of 24 hours while enrolled at Upper Iowa (a private school).

Accredited by: North Central Association of Colleges and Schools

■■■

Western Illinois University
Nontraditional Programs
5 Horrabin Hall
Macomb, IL 61455-1395
(309) 298-1929
Fax: (309) 298-2226

Degrees Offered: BA (no required major)

Credit-Earning Methods Offered/Accepted: classroom study, transfer credit, independent study, college course exams, standardized exams, prior learning/portfolio assessment, employee training, certificates and licenses, military credit, individualized study

Residency Required or External? External; you must earn 15 credits while matriculated in this degree program (through independent study or other methods).

Cost Basis/Major Costs:

- $77 per credit hour (independent study courses)
- $30 portfolio evaluation

Comments: One of the major features of this program is that there is no major requirement. You select the courses you'll need to complete 120 credits (with minimum requirements in humanities, social science, and natural science). Other requirements include upper-division courses and two political science exit exams. The cost of this degree can be very inexpensive, with only a $30 portfolio evaluation fee. (However, this program requires you to develop your plan more than at other schools.) Another great advantage is that there are no limits on how much credit you can earn through exams or portfolio examination, making this a potentially rapid degree program. If a BA will work for you, this program is worth checking out, even for those not living in Illinois. This program is offered at other locations in Illinois: Chicago State University, Eastern Illinois University, Governors State University, and Northeastern Illinois University. (Credits toward the minimum requirements can also be earned at these schools.)

Accredited by: North Central Association of Colleges and Schools

Appendix C

Accreditation

The subject of accreditation needs in-depth coverage, but an initial discussion of essential and simple points will allow you to bypass the details if you choose.

This book covers regionally accredited colleges and universities. If you had to bet your career on any sort of academic degree obtainable in the U.S., you would want a regionally accredited degree. The happy news is that you don't need to bet at all: Nontraditional students can choose from hundreds of accredited degree programs. Within these programs there are many ways to earn credit and apply it toward a degree.

The regional accrediting organizations operate in six distinct geographic areas of the U.S. A school's regional accrediting agency is determined by the state (or territory) where the school is headquartered. When you investigate a school and want to determine if it's regionally accredited, look over its materials (bulletins, catalogs, and other promotional items) to find out if the state's designated regional accrediting agency is listed under claimed accreditation; look carefully, it may be hidden or in small type. If you cannot determine if it's regionally accredited, consider it a warning. Call the school and/or contact the regional accrediting body to find out. You should determine if the regional accrediting body has accredited the whole school, or only the college or degree program you are interested in. (For simplicity, ideally the whole school is regionally accredited.) The six regional accrediting bodies are:

- Delaware, District of Columbia, Maryland, New Jersey, New York, Pennsylvania, Puerto Rico, and Virgin Islands:

  Middle States Association of Colleges and Schools
  3624 Market Street
  Philadelphia, PA 19104
  (215) 662-5606
  Fax: (215) 662-5950

- Connecticut, Maine, Massachusetts, New Hampshire, Rhode Island, and Vermont:

    New England Association of Schools and Colleges, Inc.
    The Sanborn House
    15 High Street
    Winchester, MA 01890
    (617) 729-6762
    Fax: (617) 729-0924

- Arizona, Arkansas, Colorado, Illinois, Indiana, Iowa, Kansas, Michigan, Minnesota, Missouri, Nebraska, New Mexico, North Dakota, Ohio, Oklahoma, South Dakota, West Virginia, Wisconsin, and Wyoming:

    North Central Association of Colleges and Schools
    159 North Dearborn Street
    Chicago, IL 60601
    (312) 263-0456
    Fax: (312) 263-7462

- Alaska, Idaho, Montana, Nevada, Oregon, Utah, and Washington:

    The Northwest Association of Schools and Colleges
    3700-B University Way, N.E.
    Seattle, WA 98105
    (206) 543-0195

- Alabama, Florida, Georgia, Kentucky, Louisiana, Mississippi, North Carolina, South Carolina, Tennessee, Texas, and Virginia:

    Southern Association of Colleges and Schools
    1866 Southern Lane
    Decatur, GA 30033-4097
    (404) 329-6500
    Fax: (404) 329-6598

- California, Guam, and Hawaii:

    Western Association of Schools and Colleges
    Senior Colleges and Universities
    P.O. Box 9900
    Oakland, CA 94613-0990
    (415) 632-5000
    Fax: (415) 632-8361

Western Association of Schools and Colleges
Community and Junior Colleges
P.O. Box 70
3060 Valencia Avenue
Aptos, CA 95003
(408) 688-7575
Fax: (408) 688-1841

Each regional agency accredits schools and degree programs that meet its educational standards. Schools without such an accreditation are operating out of the mainstream of higher education. You may contact any accrediting agency to find out the status of any school you're interested in. If you locate an unaccredited school and you know nothing else about it, assume a degree from that school is worthless.

Diploma Mills

Diploma mills are companies that issue worthless educational credentials. Like any business, they do this to make a profit and will employ almost any method they can to coax money out of your wallet. The hallmark of a diploma mill is the degree-for-money exchange. Diploma mills use many clever means to exude the appearance of a legitimate degree-granting school.

- They may claim accreditation by some agency other than one of the six regionals.
- They may lie and claim accreditation by a regional accrediting agency.
- They may refer to themselves as nontradtional, offer a few courses, and require thesis papers.
- They may favorably compare themselves with accredited schools whose names you know and recognize.
- They may give you beautiful brochures listing the various PhDs on their faculties.
- They may tout approval by the state board, but this is not regional accreditation. This is a favorite technique.
- They may use names that sound very much like famous schools or that in some way seem respectable.

Despite these ploys, diploma mills issue worthless degrees. You certainly can't use such a degree to get into graduate schools, and if you try to fool your employer with a phony degree, you might end up needing a good lawyer. The only beneficiary of a fake diploma is the person selling it.

Proprietors of diploma mills will either be up-front about their lack of regional accreditation or do anything to distract you from the issue. In the first case, you know where you stand. In the latter case, you must get a yes or no answer to a question such as, "Since your operation is headquartered in Alabama, are you accredited by the Southern Association of Colleges and Schools?" If the proprietor won't give you a simple yes or no, then the answer is no. If you get a yes and still feel suspicious, call the accrediting body.

Specialized Accrediting Bodies

Certain graduate schools give preference to (or require) applicants who hold degrees from schools with specialized accreditation in addition to regional accreditation. If you want to pursue a bachelor's degree and are already thinking about a particular school for a master's degree, determine if the graduate school has admission requirements pertaining to specialized accreditation. If possible, ask before you matriculate in the undergraduate degree program.

If you plan on entering an engineering profession involving life, health, or property, or if you intend to offer your services to the public, you must register with the state where you work or reside. Part of the requirement for registry is a degree from an engineering program accredited by the Accreditation Board for Engineering and Technology. In the various engineering specialties (not just high-technology ones), approximately one-third of engineers are registered.

The specialized accrediting bodies hold degree programs (such as electronics) to additional standards such as core curriculum courses. Not all graduate schools have these requirements, but students who need degrees with specialized accreditation must make sure their schools actually have this additional accreditation and not programs that merely conform to specialized accrediting standards. When in doubt, contact the school and the specialized accrediting body.

Specialized accrediting bodies of interest to the technical professions are:

Accreditation Board for Engineering and Technology
345 East 47th Street
New York, NY 10017
(212) 705-7685
Fax: (212) 838-8062

Computer Sciences Accreditation Commission
345 East 47th Street
New York, NY 10017
(212) 705-7314
Fax: (212) 371-9622

Nontradtional or Unaccredited?

Don't be confused by these terms. If you're interested in a nontradtional school, you're also interested in a regionally accredited school that has some nontraditional features. Since the term *nontraditional* has been commonly used to describe alternative programs from regionally accredited schools, some diploma mills have described their operations as nontraditional in a further attempt to legitimize themselves. Don't be fooled.

Trade and Technical Schools

The learning programs at legitimate trade and technical schools are not meant to prepare students for the professional-level high-technology careers described in this book. You should look at claims contrary to this with suspicion. Trade schools may have a different type of accreditation from the National Association of Technical and Trade Schools (NATTS), which is not regional accreditation, not equivalent to regional accreditation, and not a substitute for regional accreditation. It's a different type of accreditation altogether.

The Bottom Line

Not only must you watch out for degree mills, you must also be aware that when standards at an accredited school drop, its regional accreditation may be suspended or taken away. Double-check before you matriculate that any school in this book is still in good standing, isn't suspended, and isn't under investigation. Accept no substitute for accreditation by one of the six regional accrediting agencies.

Obtaining a
High School Diploma

This book assumes that you already have a high school diploma. For instance, your high school transcript is considered part of the documentation you need to submit with your college admission application. If you don't have a high school diploma, you can either complete it or try to gain college admission without it.

Some colleges will, as an exception, accept students without a high school diploma. They usually require the student to clear a few hurdles designed to prove high school level skills. One way to demonstrate these skills is to take a variety of college-level courses at a community college or to enroll in a continuing education program offered by a local four-year school. Often, a high school diploma isn't required to enroll in these courses.

Another way to earn college credit is to complete college-level independent study courses. Check with colleges you are considering to ask them about their diploma policies. You'll need to plan an appropriate strategy to meet the college's acceptance criteria.

You can obtain high school credentials in several ways.

- You can pass the GED high school equivalency exam. Contact a local high school, adult education center, or public library to find out about this popular option. Many cities offer training classes in addition to the exams. Many study guides are available for the GED exam.

- You can earn a high school diploma through the mail. Contact the following four accredited schools for more information.

Home Study International
6940 Carroll Avenue
Takoma Park, Maryland 20912
(202) 722-6572

American School
850 East 58th Street
Chicago, IL 60637
(312) 947-3300

Brigham Young University
Independent Study
206 Harmon
Provo, Utah 84602
(801) 378-2868

University of Nebraska
269 Nebraska Center for Continuing Education
33rd and Holdrege Streets
Lincoln, NE 68583-0900
(402) 472-1926

- You can go back to high school by registering with the principal to start classes. You may also earn high school credit by enrolling at a local school and taking courses through the mail. (To find high school correspondence courses, use Peterson's *Independent Study Catalog*.)

Career and Job-Hunting Information Leads

Career Information

A good place to collect information is from the people closest to you, your family and friends. Personal contacts are often over-looked, but can be extremely helpful. They may be able to answer your questions directly or, more importantly, put you in touch with someone else who can. Your networking may lead to an informational interview where you can meet with someone willing to answer your questions about a career or a company. This person may provide inside information on related fields and other helpful hints. This is an effective way for you to learn the recommended type of training for a particular position and find out how to enter and advance in that position. You also will find what your contact likes and dislikes about the work. While developing your network of contacts, you may want to begin exploring other avenues.

Public libraries, career centers, and guidance offices have a great deal of career material. To begin your library search, look in the card catalog or at the computer listings for vocations, careers, or specific fields. Also leaf through pamphlets that describe employment in different organizations. Check the periodicals section for trade and professional magazines and journals about specific occupations and industries. Familiarize yourself with the concerns and activities of potential employers by skimming their annual reports and other publicly distributed information.

You can also find occupation information on videocassettes, in kits, and through computerized information systems. Check career centers for programs such as individual counseling, group discussions, guest speakers, field trips, and career days.

Always assess career-guidance materials carefully. Information should be current. Beware of school-recruitment materials that glamorize an occupation, overstate its earnings, or exaggerate its demand for workers.

You may want to seek help from a counselor. Counselors are trained to help you discover your strengths and weaknesses, evaluate your goals and values, and determine what you want in a career. The counselor won't tell you what to do, but administers interest inventories and aptitude tests, interprets the results, and helps you explore your options. Counselors also may be able to discuss local job markets as well as the entry requirements and costs of the schools, colleges, and training programs that offer preparations for your desired field. You can find counselors in:

- High school guidance offices
- College career planning and placement offices
- Placement offices in private vocational/technical schools and institutions
- Counseling services offered by community organizations
- Private counseling agencies and practices
- State employment service offices affiliated with the U.S. Employment Service

Before employing the services of a private counselor or agency, you should seek recommendations and check credentials. The International Association of Counseling Services (IACS) accredits counseling services throughout the country. To receive the listing of services for your region contact IACS, 101 South Whiting Street, Suite 211, Alexandria, VA 22304. The IACS publication *The Directory of Counseling Services* may be available at your library or career counseling center. For a list of certified career counselors by state, contact the National Board of Certified Counselors at (919) 547-0607.

Professional societies, trade associations, labor unions, business firms, and educational institutions provide a variety of free or inexpensive career materials. Look under specific occupations in the Sources of Additional Information section of the *Occupational Outlook Handbook*. The *Handbook* also lists contact information for state occupational information-coordinating committees, which can provide you with other career information at the state and local level.

Job-Hunting Information

Many people require a great deal of time and effort to find an enjoyable job. Others walk right into an ideal job. Don't be discouraged if you have to pursue many leads. Friends, neighbors, teachers, and counselors may know of available jobs in your field of interest. Read the want ads. Consult state employment service offices and private or nonprofit employment agencies, or contact employers directly.

WHERE TO FIND JOB OPENINGS

- State employment service offices
- Civil service announcements (federal, state, and local)
- Classified ads
  - Local and out-of-town newspapers
  - Professional journals
  - Trade magazines
- Labor unions
- Professional associations (state and local chapters)
- Libraries and community centers
- Women's counseling and employment programs
- Youth programs
- School or college placement services
- Employment agencies and career consultants
- Employers
- Parents, friends, and neighbors

Tips for Finding the Right Job, a U.S. Department of Labor pamphlet, offers advice on determining your job skills, organizing your job search, writing a résumé, and making the most of an interview. Check with your state employment service office, or order a copy from the Superintendent of Documents by phoning (202) 783-3238.

Getting Back to Work, a Department of Labor booklet, helps laid-off workers in particular. It provides information on searching for and landing a job in addition to detailing 250 occupations most likely to require the skills of displaced workers. This booklet is available free of charge at most state employment service offices or can be ordered directly from the Department of Labor by phoning (202) 272-5381.

Informal Job Search Methods

You can apply directly to employers without a referral. Locate potential employers in the Yellow Pages and in directories of local chambers of commerce.

Want Ads

Newspaper ads list hundreds of jobs. However, many job openings aren't listed there. Also, be aware that classified ads often don't give important information. Many offer little or no description of the job, working conditions, or pay. Some ads don't identify the employer. This makes follow up difficult. Furthermore, some ads offer out-of-town jobs, while others advertise employment agencies rather than actual jobs.

Keep the following in mind when you use want ads.

- Don't rely solely on the classifieds to find a job; follow other leads as well.
- Answer ads promptly.
- Follow the ads diligently. Check them every day, as early as possible, to give yourself an advantage.
- Keep a record of all ads to which you've responded.

Organizations for Specific Groups

Many organizations provide information on career planning and employment for women, minorities, veterans, the disabled, and older workers. For contact information about these various groups, see the Leads to More Information section of the *Occupational Outlook Handbook*.

Help from University Degree Advisory

University Degree Advisory (UDA) is a business founded to promote nontraditional degree alternatives. Much of the information in this book comes from the accumulated experience of operating this business to the satisfaction of thousands of individuals. UDA offers two valuable services for clients.

Individual Consulting

This service assists would-be students in selecting schools and developing preliminary degree completion plans. UDA gathers extensive information by mail, then follows up with a phone interview (if necessary). Following analysis, UDA produces and mails out a report.

If you've worked through the information in this book, you've essentially produced your own report (and more), but you may want additional professional advice on creating a very aggressive degree completion plan.

UDA produces its report in two to five weeks, and the price is moderately expensive compared to the cost of this book.

Corporate Consulting and Group Training

Corporate clients can take advantage of various services designed to encourage employees to investigate degree alternatives. Half- or full-day UDA training sessions quickly familiarize employees with alternative degree concepts and get them started on finishing their degrees. Consulting sessions with human resource personnel are also offered to educate corporate employees, who can then promote college degrees in their own training programs.

For more information about these services, write to UDA at the following address.

University Degree Advisory
P.O. Box 2234
Eugene, OR 97402

Bibliography and Resources

Guides to Colleges and Universities

The books listed in this section are directories to colleges and universities in the U.S., but the list is far from comprehensive. Should you need to use such a guide, check your public library, local high school library, or counseling office for a copy.

- The College Board. *The College Handbook*. New York, 1993.

- Parnell, Dale and J.W. Peltason. *American Community, Technical and Junior Colleges*, 9th ed. Washington: ACE/Macmillan, 1986.

- Peterson's Guides. *Peterson's Guide to Four Year Colleges*, 23d ed. Princeton, NJ, 1993.

- Straughn, Charles T. and Barbara Sue Straughn. *Lovejoy's College Guide*, 20th ed. New York: Prentice-Hall, 1991.

- Yellow Page business directories are published by your local phone company and other businesses.

Independent Study Guides and Resources

- Macmillan Publishing Company. *The Macmillan Guide to Correspondence Study*. New York, 1983.

- Mind Extension University (Cable TV)
  P.O. Box 3309
  Englewood, CO 80155-3309
  1-800-777-6463

- Peterson's Guides. *The Independent Study Catalog*, 5th ed. Princeton, NJ, 1992.

- University of Phoenix, On Line
  101 California Street, Suite 505
  San Francisco, CA 94111
  (415) 956-2121

Standardized Examination Preparation

- ARCO AP Prepatory Books
  Separate publications for biology, calculus, computer science, English, American history.
  Published by Simon and Schuster, New York.

- ARCO GRE Prepatory Series
  Various titles for different exams; contains detailed solutions and test-taking techniques.
  Published by Simon and Schuster, New York.

- College Board Publications. *The Official Handbook for the CLEP Examinations*. New York, 1992.

- Practicing to Take the GRE Subject Exam Series
  Various titles for different exams.
  Published by Warner Books and ETS, New York.

Ponsi Directories (for Training Credit)

- American Council on Education. *The National Guide to Educational Credit for Training Programs*. Washington, 1990.

- State University of New York. *College Credit Recommendations: The Directory of The National Program on Noncollegiate Sponsored Instruction*, 6th ed. New York, 1992.

Prior Learning Credit and Portfolio Evaluation

- Lamdin, Lois. *Earn College Credit For What You Know*, 2nd ed. Chicago: Council for Adult and Experiential Learning, 1992.

Financial Aid

You will find many good books available to guide you through the maze of financial aid terminology, sources, and the financial aid process. The following are two valuable guides you can look for at your library.

- *Lovejoy's Guide To Financial Aid*, 3rd ed. New York: Prentice-Hall, 1989.

- Peterson's Guides. *Peterson's College Money Handbook*, 9th ed. Princeton, NJ, 1992.

Page numbers in italic indicate material found in sidebars.

AARTS. *See* Army/ACE Registry Transcript Service
Academic advisors, *26*
Accreditation, 163–167
Accreditation Board for Engineering and Technology, 166
Accredited, 123
Accredited nontraditional education, 3–4, 13–21
Accrediting bodies, 166
ACE. *See* American Council on Education
ACE PONSI. *See* American Council on Education PONSI
ACP. *See* Associate Computer Professional
ACT PEP. *See* American College Testing Proficiency Examination Program
ACT PEP Candidate Registration Guide, 54
ACT PEP exams, 53–55
Admission process, 107–111, 123
Advanced Placement Exams (AP), 44, 49–50, 123
After graduation, self-promotion, 119–121
Agents, college, 110–111
Age restrictions, *28*
American College Testing Proficiency Examination Program (ACT PEP), 53–55, 123
American Community Technical and Junior Colleges, 177
American Council on Education (ACE), 60, 123
American Council on Education PONSI, 60
American School, 170
Antioch University, 126
AP. *See* Advanced Placement Exams
ARCO AP Preparatory Books, 178
ARCO GRE Preparatory Series, 178
Army/ACE Registry Transcript Service (AARTS), 64, 123
Arts degree, 8

Associate computer professional (ACP), *64*
Associate of Science Degree, 16
Associate's degree, 123
Atlantic Union College, 127
Aviation licenses and certificates, *64–65*

Baccalaureate degree, 123
Bachelor of Science Degree, 16
Bachelor's degree, 123
Bradley University, 128
Brigham Young University, 37, 128, 170
Burlington College, 129
Business certificates, *64*

Cable study, *33*
CAEL. *See* Council for Adult and Experiential Learning
Capital University, 129
Career goals, 9–10
Career information, 171–172
CDP. *See* Certified data processor
CEBS. *See* Certified employee benefit specialist
CEEB, 123
Central Michigan University, 130
Certificate in Computer Programming (ICCP), *64*
Certificates, 17–18, 62–64
Certified data processor (CDP), *64*
Certified employee benefit specialist (CEBS), *64*
Certified financial planner (CFP), *64*
Certified professional secretary (CPS), *64*
Certified public accountant (CPA), *64*
Certified Public Manager Program of New Jersey (CPM), *64*
Certified purchasing manager (CPM), *64*
Certified systems professional (CSP), *64*
CFP. *See* Certified financial planner
Challenge exams, 39–42, 123

Charter Oak State College, 131
Chartered financial consultant (ChFC), *64*
Chartered life underwriter (CLU), *64*
Chartered property casualty underwriter (CPCU), *64*
ChFC. *See* Chartered financial consultant
Choosing a degree, 7–10
Choosing the right school, 83–92
City University, 132
CLEP. *See* College Level Examination Program
CLU. *See* Chartered life underwriter
College agents, 110–111
College course examinations, 17
College credit
  estimating, 80
  for experience, 69–73
  from training, 59–67
  inventory existing, 98
  military training, 64–67
  other ways, 15–18
College Credit Recommendations: The Directory of The National Program on Noncollegiate Sponsored Instruction, 60, 178
College degree benefits, *6*
College Handbook, The, 177
College Level Examination Program (CLEP), 17, 43–44, 47–49, 123
College materials, evaluating, 84
Colorado State University, 133
Columbia Union College, 133
Commencement, 123
Community College of the Air Force, 65
Company-sponsored education, 17
Computer Sciences Accreditation Commission, 166
Contacting colleges and universities, *84*
COPA. *See* Council on Postsecondary Accreditation
Correspondence instruction, 33
Costs, calculating, 105
Council for Adult and Experiential Learning (CAEL), *72*, 123

Council on Postsecondary Accreditation (COPA), 17, 28, *29*, 123
CPA. *See* Certified public
accountant
CPCU. *See* Chartered property
casualty underwriter
CPM. *See* Certified purchasing
manager
CPS. *See* Certified professional
secretary
Crashing, *120*
Credentials, 123
Credit
bank, 21, 123
building methods, 79–82
by examination, 39–57
inventory, 100–105
transfers, 27–31
CSP. *See* Certified systems
professional

DA Form 2-1, 65–66
DA Form 5454-R, 64
DANTES. *See* Defense Activity
for Non-Traditional Education
Support
DANTES Standardized Subject
Tests (DSST), 55–56
DD Form 214, 64
DD Form 295, 64
Deadlines, 10–11
Defense Activity for Non-Tradi-
tional Education Support
(DANTES), 35, 55–56, 123
Defining underlying goals, 5–7
Degree
completion time, 39–57
costs, 87–89, 105
increased income, 7
individualized programs, 75–77
matching career goals, 9–10
needed, 5–11
nontraditional schools, 13–18
plan, 113–117
program requirements, 15–16
sketch, 93–106
Departmental exams, 123. *See
also* Challenge exams
*Directory of Counseling Services,
The,* 172
Diploma, 123
Diploma mills, 123, 165–166
Doctor of Philosophy (PhD), 124

Driver training, *104*
DSST. *See* DANTES Standardized
Subject Tests

Eastern Oregon State College, 134
Eastern West Virginia State
University, 20
Edison State College, 135
Educational credential, 8–10
Educational Testing Service
(ETS), 55
Electives, 123
Elizabethtown College, 135
Embry-Riddle Aeronautical
University, 136
Empire State College, 137
Employee training, 17
English requirements, 100
Enrollment, 18, 124
ETS. *See* Educational Testing
Service
Evelyn Wood Reading Dynamics, *65*
Evergreen State College, 137
Examinations, 40, 56–57
Experiential, 124
External schools, 20–21

FAA. *See* Federal Aviation
Administration
FAA airplane transport pilot, *64*
FAA air traffic control specialist, *64*
FAA flight engineer, *64*
FAA instructor, *64*
FAA mechanic rating for airframe
and/or power plant, *64*
FAA multiengine airplane, *64*
FAA pilot airplane, *65*
FAA rotocraft pilot, *65*
Federal Aviation Administration
(FAA), 62
Filled classes, *24*
Financial aid, 88–91, 178
Foreign transcripts, *30*
Future credit transfers, *31*
Future training credits, *61*

General education, 124
Getting Back to Work, 173
GPA. *See* Grade point average
Grade point average (GPA), 24, 124
Graded exams, 40
Graduate, 124

Graduate Record Examination
(GRE), 17, 44–45, 51–53, 124
GRE. *See* Graduate Record
Examination
GSA/National Personnel Records
Center, 64
*Guide to the Advanced Place-
ment Program,* 50
*Guide to the Evaluation of
Educational Experiences in the
Armed Services,* 65

*Higher Education Opportunities
for Minorities and Women,* 89
High school diploma, 169–170
Histotechnology, *65*
Home Study International, 169

IACS. *See* International
Association of Counseling
Services
Independent study, 16–17, 33–38,
124, 170
Independent Study Catalog, 170,
177
Indiana Institute of Technology, 138
Indiana University, 139
Individual Duty Area Qualification
Summary Sheet, 65
Individualized degree programs, 18,
75–77, 124
International Association of
Counseling Services (IACS), 172

Job-hunting information, 172–173
Johnson State College, 139

Laboratory, 124
Liberal arts, 124
Licenses, 17–18, 62–64
Loans, 90
Lovejoy's College Guide, 177
*Lovejoy's Guide To Financial
Aid,* 178
Lower division, 124

*Macmillan Guide to Correspond-
ence Study, The,* 177
Major, 124
Mary Baldwin College, 140
Master of Business Administra-
tion (MBA), 124
Master of Science degree, 16

Master's degree, 124
Matriculation, 18, 124
MBA. *See* Master of Business
    Administration
ME/U. *See* Mind Extension
    University
Medical licenses, 65
Middle States Association of
    Colleges and Schools, 163
Military credit, 18, *66*
Military forms. *See* DA Form 2-1,
    DA Form 66, DA Form 5454-R,
    DD Form 214, DD Form 295,
    USAEEC Form 10A
Military training credit, 64–67
Mind Extension University
    (ME/U), 36, 141, 177
Minor, 124
Miscellaneous licenses and
    certificates, *65*
Motivation, *8*

National Association of Techni-
    cal and Trade Schools
    (NATTS), *29*, 124
National Board of Certified
    Counselors, 172
*National Guide to Educational
    Credit for Training Programs,
    The*, 60, 178
*National Home Study Council
    (NHSC)*, *29*, 124
National PONSI. *See* National
    Program on Noncollegiate
    Sponsored Instruction
National Program on Noncollegiate
    Sponsored Instruction (National
    PONSI), *60*, 178
National Registry of Radiation
    Protection Technologies, *65*
National Technological Univer-
    sity, 141
NATTS. *See* National Associa-
    tion of Technical and Trade
    Schools
Navy Nuclear Power School, *65*
New England Association of
    Schools and Colleges, Inc., 164
New Jersey EMT ambulance, *65*
New Jersey EMT paramedic, *65*
New York Institute of Technology,
    37, 142
New York University Proficiency
    Testing in Foreign Language, 56

NHSC. *See* National Home Study
    Council
Nontraditional schools, 13–21, 167
North Central Association of
    Colleges and Schools, 164
Northwest Association of Schools
    and Colleges, 164
Northwood Institute, 142
Nova University, 143
NRC reactor operator, *65*
NRC senior reactor operator, *65*
Nuclear certificates and licenses, *65*
Nuclear medicine technology, *65*

Occupational Outlook Handbook,
    9–10, 172
*Official Handbook for the CLEP
    Examinations, The*, 178
Ohio University, 41, 144
Oklahoma City University, 145
On-line classes, 35

PACE. *See* Program for Adult
    College Education
Pace University, 145
Pass/fail, 24–25
Pass/no-pass, 24
Pennsylvania State University, 146
*Peterson's College Money Hand-
    book*, 178
*Peterson's Guide to Four Year
    Colleges*, 177
PhD. *See* Doctor of Philosophy
PONSI. *See* Programs on Nucolle-
    giate Sponsored Instruction
Portfolio evaluation, 17, 178
*Preparing to Do Your Best on the
    ACT PEP Examination*, 54
Prerequisite, 124
Prescott College, 146
Prior learning credit, 17, *69*, 124
Proctors, *34*
Program for Adult College Educa-
    tion (PACE), 25
Programs on Noncollegiate Spon-
    sored Instruction (PONSI), *59*
Publications, assessing prior
    learning, *72*

Quarter, 124
Quarter credit hour system, 29–30

Radiation therapy technology, *65*
Radiologic technology, *65*
RCE. *See* Regents College Exams

Regents College Exams (RCE), 124
Registered nurse, 65
Registrar, 124
Regis University, 147
Required-residency schools, 19–20
Requirements, elective, 99–100
Residency, in military, *87*
Respiratory therapist, 65
Respiratory therapy technician, 65
Roger Williams College, 147

St. Edwards University, 148
SAT. *See* Scholastic Achievement
    Test
Scholastic Achievement Test (SAT),
    42
School, choosing, 83–92
School bulletins, *125*
Science degree, 8
Self-motivation, *37*
Self-promotion, after graduation,
    119–121
Semester, 124
Semester/quarter credit hour
    systems, 29–30
Setting initial deadlines, 10–11
Skidmore College, 149
Southern Association of Colleges
    and Schools, 164
Stale credits. *See* Age restrictions
Stand and Deliver, 49
Standardized examinations, 17,
    41–57, 178
Stephens Colleges, 149
Study-by-mail, 17, 33
SUNY Empire State College
    External Programs Bookstore, 55
Superintendent of documents, 173
Surveyor license, *65*
Syracuse University, 150

TECEP. *See* Thomas Edison
    College Examination Program
Technical schools, credit, *29*
Technology degrees, 1–11
Therapy licenses, *65*
Thomas Edison College Examina-
    tion Program (TECEP), 41
Thomas Edison State College, 41
Time restrictions. *See* Age restric-
    tions
Tips for Finding the Right Job, 173
TOCT, 57

Total quality management (TQM) techniques, 70
TQM. *See* Total quality management techniques
Trade schools, *29*, 167
Traditional classroom study, 23–26
Transcript
  defined, 124
  foreign, *30*
  postscripts, *108*
  sending, *28*
  services, *60*
Transferring credit, 15–16
Trinity College, 150
Troy State University, 151

UDA. *See* University Degree Advisory
Undergraduate, 124

Union Institute, 152
University of Alabama, 152
University Degree Advisory (UDA), 176
University of Evansville, 153
University of Idaho, 154
University of Maryland, 155
University of Massachusetts, 155–157
University of Michigan, 37
University of Minnesota, 157
University of Nebraska, 170
University of Oklahoma, 158
University of Phoenix Online, 36, 177
University of South Florida, 158
University of the State of New York, 159
University of Wisconsin-Madison, 160

Upper division, 124
Upper Iowa University, 160
USAEEC Form 10A, 64
U.S. Department of Labor, 173

VCR. *See* Video cassette recorder
Video cassette recorder (VCR), *33*, 36, 124
Video tapes, 35

Western Association of Schools and Colleges: Community and Junior Colleges, 165
Western Association of Schools and Colleges: Senior Colleges and Universities, 164
Western Illinois University, 161